The 10-Part Agenda for the Last Supper with Jesus

For Youth Groups, Jesus Lovers, Church Leaders, Bible Study Groups, and Families eager for a deeper understanding of our Lord Jesus Christ
(Study Guide Included)

Debbie Dunn

© 2024 by Debbie Dunn. All rights reserved.

FYI - Unless otherwise noted, most Biblical quotes come from either the King James Version (KJV) or the New International Version (NIV) of the Bible APP.

<u>Permissions</u>: This book or any portion thereof may not be reproduced or used in any manner without the publisher's express written permission except for using brief quotations in a book review. For copy permission, please email the author, Debbie Dunn, at moredunntales@yahoo.com. Place, in the subject line: **Ten-part Agenda for Last Supper with Jesus**

<u>Disclaimer</u>: The content used in this book is intended for educational and informational purposes only.

ISBN: 9798227487315

Imprint: Independently published. Distributed by Draft 2 Digital

T.R.E.A.T. Tales Presents

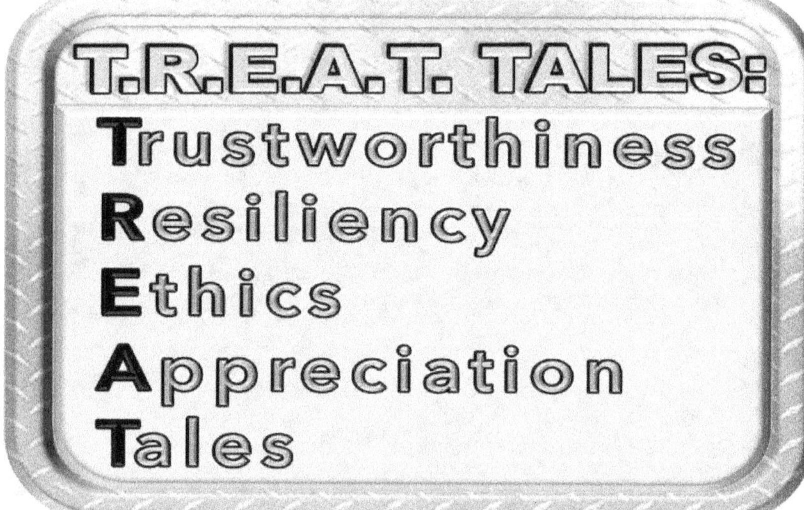

Website: https://bible-books-for-his-glory.com/index.html
Email: moredunntales@yahoo.com

About the Author: Debbie Dunn

Debbie Dunn has been a professional storyteller since 1989. She has also taught at-risk teens, served as an anti-bullying specialist, and taught elementary and middle school. In her retirement years, she indulges her love of our Lord Jesus Christ, nature, traveling, and writing as she pursues learning and exploring more about the Holy Bible.

Table of Contents

About the Book

Ten-part Agenda for Last Supper with Jesus is a book crafted for youth groups, Jesus lovers, church leaders, Bible study groups, and families who are eager for a deeper understanding of our Lord Jesus Christ. The author, understanding the unique needs of these groups, has filled this book with conceptual illustrations that will resonate with them, and has included a study guide for their convenience.

The ten-part agenda of the Last Supper with Jesus describes:

(1) The Last Supper occurred in an Upper Room in Jerusalem.

(2) Jesus and His Disciples reclined rather than sat at the table.

(3) Jesus was intensely aware of these final hours with His Disciples.

(4) Jesus washed His Disciples' feet.

(5) Jesus revealed that He was going to be betrayed by Judas Iscariot.

(6) Jesus introduced the Disciples to the symbolic use of bread and wine at this first-ever Holy Communion.

(7) Jesus revealed they only had a short time left together before His death.

(8) Jesus told Peter, "You will deny me three times before the cock crows."

(9) The 12 Disciples tried to get Jesus to reveal which one of them was the greatest of the twelve.

(10) Jesus described in detail the Spiritual Warfare that the Disciples would face after His death and resurrection.

This book also covers details about King David's Remez hidden messages pointing to Christ, attributes and benefits of the Holy Spirit, the Disciples' mission trip from earlier in Jesus' ministry, Jesus' feeding of the 5000, Disciple Peter's eventual martyrdom in 64 AD, and the importance of responding like Jesus rather than allowing Satan to dominate.

Fifty percent (50%) of all book sales will be donated to **Covenant House** to "***join the fight to end youth homelessness***."

FYI – This is a stand-alone book pulled from four sections of my 75-chapter book titled, "Jesus' Crucifixion and Resurrection foretold by 12 Biblical Prophets & Kings." Those four sections include:

Ten-part Agenda for Last Supper … Book	*Jesus' Crucifixion and Resurrection … Book*
Chapter 1 of this book is the same as	*Chapter 5 of my other book.*
Study Guide for Chapter 1 is the same as	*Study Guide for Chapter 5 of my other book.*
Chapter 2 is the same as	*Chapter 74 of my other book.*
Chapter 3 is a shortened Bibliography	*found in Chapter 75 of my other book.*

In **Matthew 26:17-19**, **Mark 14:12-16**, and **Luke 22:7-13** , we learned it was the first day of the **Festival of the Unleavened Bread**. How did that festival differ from **Passover Seder**?

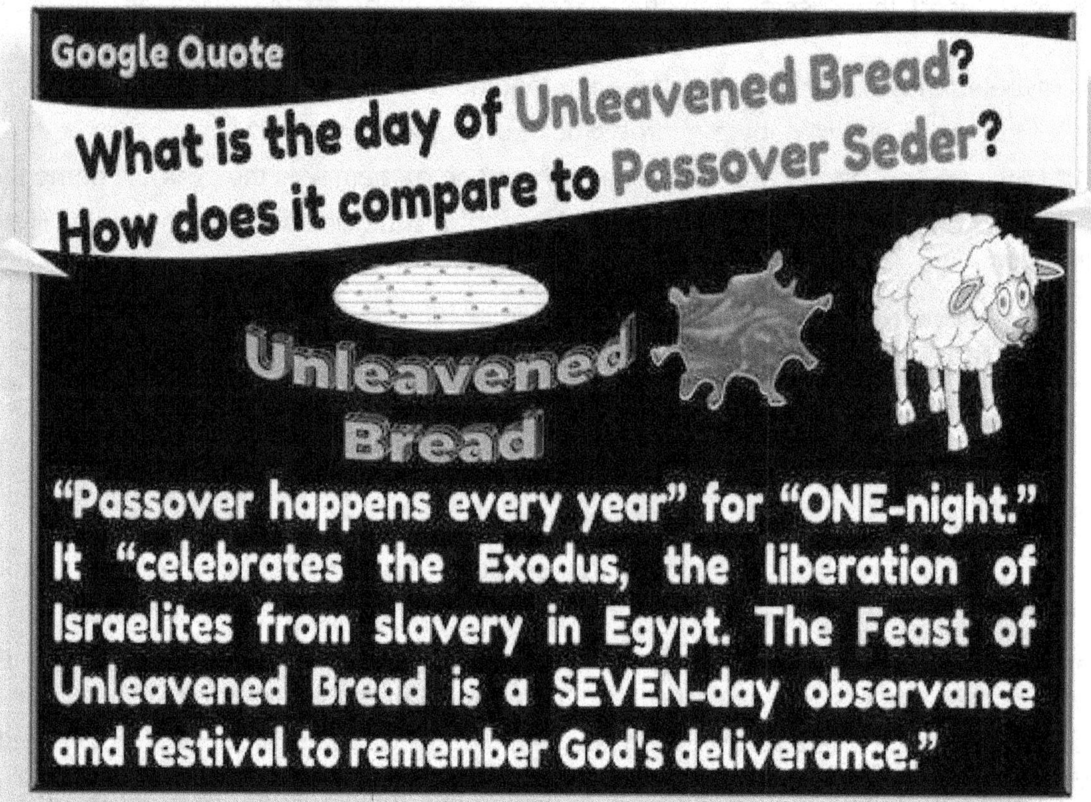

MOSES
Lamb's Blood
Passover
"Passover commemorates the slavery of the Israelites in Egypt and their ultimate exodus to freedom." Google Quote

Luke 22:8 Jesus sent Peter and John, saying, "Go and make preparations for us to eat the Passover."

Luke 22:9 "Where do you want us to prepare for it?" they asked.

Luke 22:10 He replied, "As you enter the city, a man carrying a jar of water will meet you. Follow him to the house that he enters,

Luke 22:11 and say to the owner of the house, 'The Teacher asks: Where is the guest room, where I may eat the Passover with my disciples?'

Luke 22:12 He will show you a large room upstairs, all furnished. Make preparations there."

Luke 22:13 They left and found things just as Jesus had told them. So, they prepared the Passover. (NIV)

Even those unfamiliar with celebrating the Passover Seder know that, at the very least, Peter and John had to make sure these preparations included unleavened bread, cups, and a pitcher of red wine.

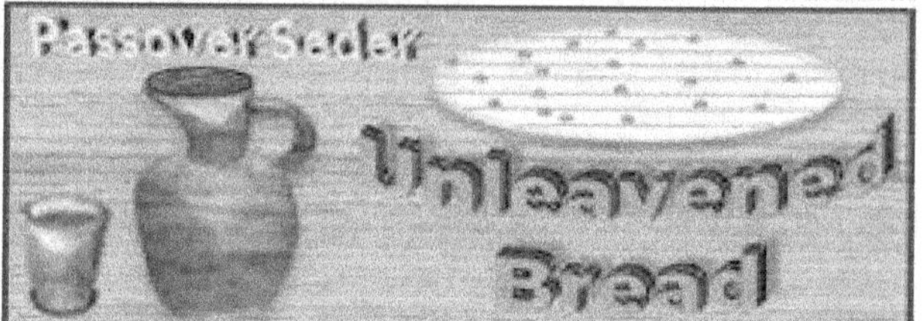

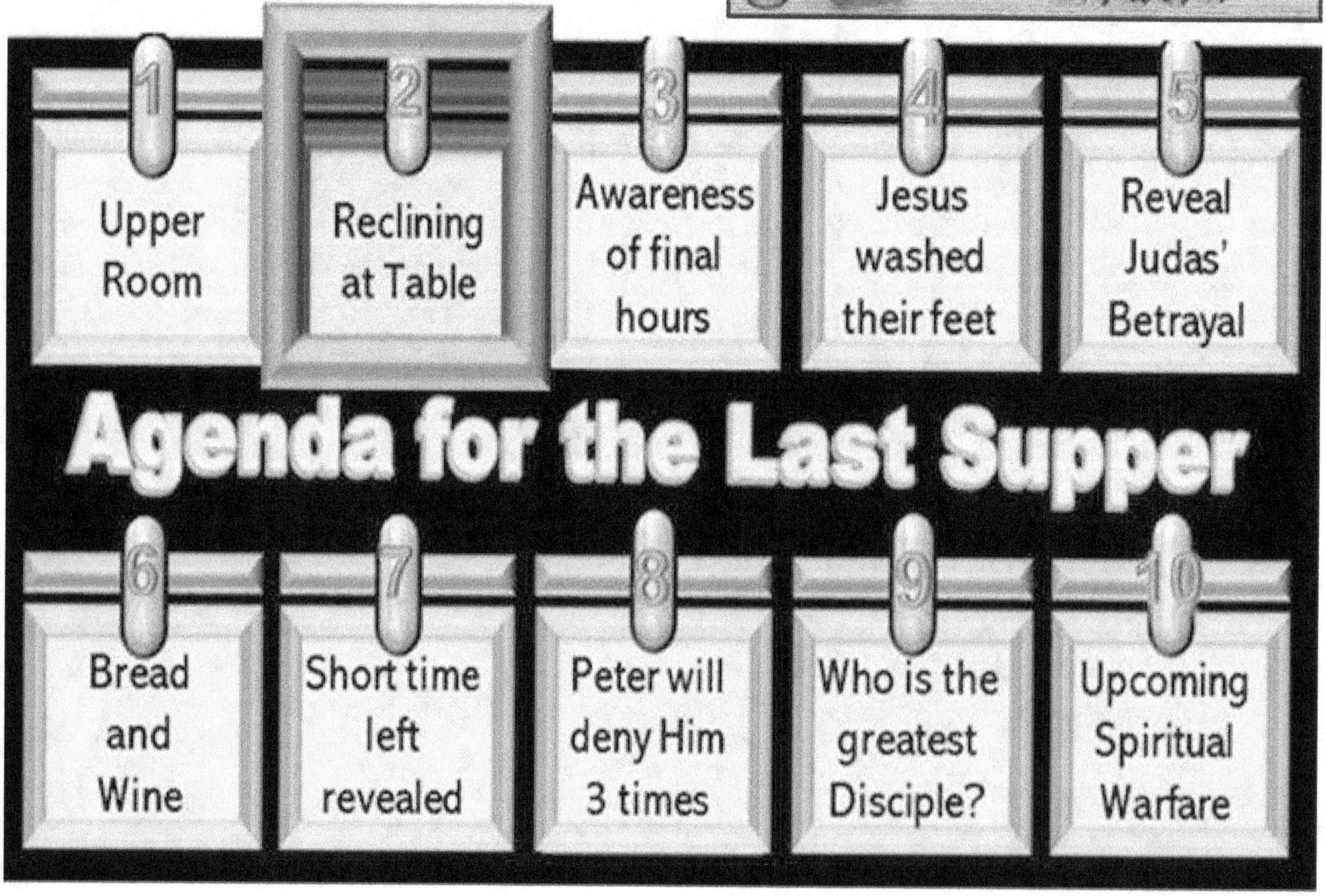

Passover Seder
Unleavened
Bread

1
Upper Room
2
Reclining at Table
3
Awareness of final hours
4
Jesus washed their feet
5
Reveal Judas' Betrayal
Agenda for the Last Supper
6
Bread and Wine
7
Short time left revealed
8
Peter will deny Him 3 times
9
Who is the greatest Disciple?
10
Upcoming Spiritual Warfare

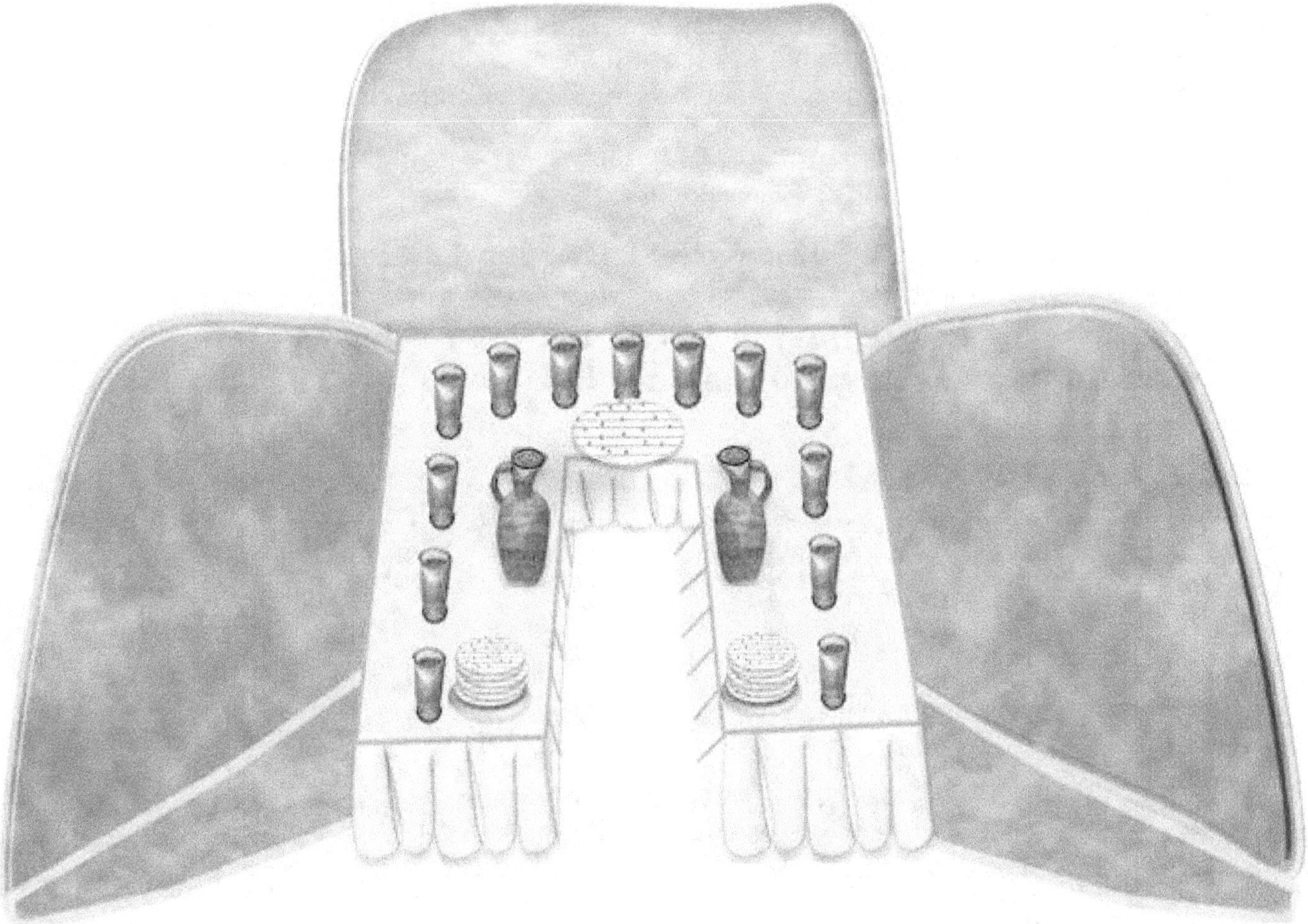

As described in **Matthew 26:20**, **Mark 14:17-18A**, and **Luke 22:14**, Jesus reclined at the table along with His twelve Disciples in this Upper Room.

It must have been bittersweet for Jesus to celebrate this Last Supper with His twelve Disciples. Even though He had hinted to them more than once that the end was near, only He knew that this night would be the last time He would spend with them as a living man.

After that night, the next time He would see them would be from the other side of the grave. In **John 13:1**, this is how Disciple John described it:

John 13:1 It was just before the Passover Festival. Jesus knew that the hour had come for him to leave this world and go to the Father. Having loved his own who were in the world, he loved them to the end. (NIV)

As previously discussed, Jesus did not fit Judas' boxed-in view of a Messiah. Due to this disenchantment with his former hero, he had determined to force Jesus to finally fight against the Romans or be sanctioned by the Sanhedrin.

The Sanhedrin had already happily handed Judas thirty pieces of silver as payment for this betrayal. Judas watched for the ideal moment to act.

Naturally, Jesus was aware of the plans of His soon-to-be-former Disciple. Judas might have thought he was choosing the time. Instead, Jesus chose their Passover Seder meal to force Judas to either recant from or follow through on his evil intentions.

Aware of Judas' betrayal plans, Jesus still intended to wash his feet.

Which side of fence did Judas choose?

John 13:3 Jesus knew that the Father had put all things under his power, and that he had come from God and was returning to God; 4 so he got up from the meal, took off his outer clothing, and wrapped a towel around his waist. 5 After that, he poured water into a basin and began to wash his disciples' feet, drying them with the towel that was wrapped around him. (NIV)

Apostle Peter said:

Jesus said:

John 13:6 He came to Simon Peter, who said to him, "Lord, are you going to wash my feet?"

John 13:7 Jesus replied, "You do not realize now what I am doing, but later you will understand."

John 13:8A "No," said Peter, "you shall never wash my feet."

John 13:8B Jesus answered, "Unless I wash you, you have no part with me."

Apostle Peter said:

John 13:9 "Then, Lord," Simon Peter replied, "not just my feet but my hands and my head as well!"

John 13:10 Jesus answered, "Those who have had a bath need only to wash their feet; their whole body is clean. And you are clean, though not every one of you."

John 13:11 For he knew who was going to betray him, and that was why he said not every one was clean. (NIV)

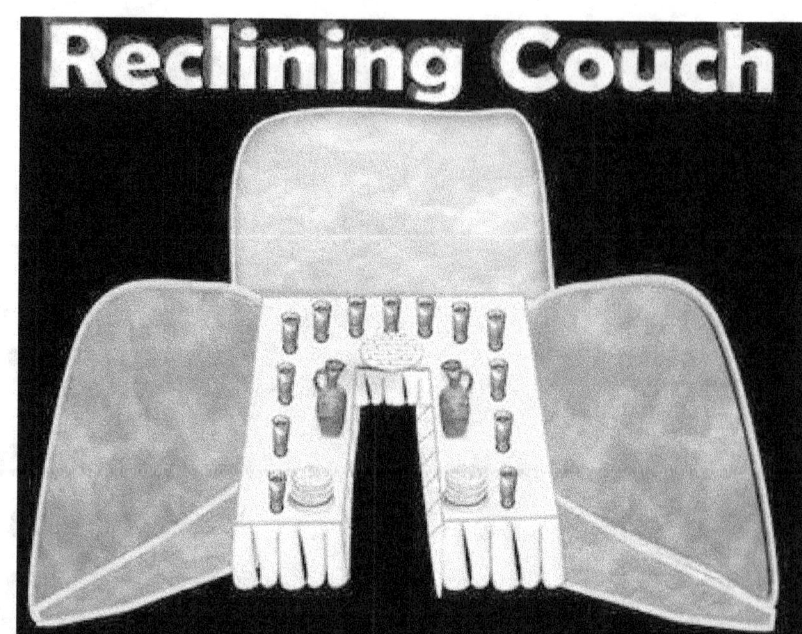

John 13:12 **When he had finished washing their feet, he put on his clothes and returned to his place. "Do you understand what I have done for you?" he asked them.**

John 13:13 **"You call me 'Teacher' and 'Lord,' and rightly so, for that is what I am.**

John 13:14 **Now that I, your Lord and Teacher, have washed your feet, you also should wash one another's feet.**

John 13:15 **I have set you an example that you should do as I have done for you.**

John 13:16 **Very truly I tell you, no servant is greater than his master, nor is a messenger greater than the one who sent him. 17 Now that you know these things, you will be blessed if you do them."**
(NIV)

The time had come for Jesus to share what would happen with Judas Iscariot. He began this testimony with the following words:

John 13:18 "I am not referring to all of you; I know those I have chosen. But this is to fulfill this passage of Scripture: 'He who shared my bread has turned against me.'   **(NIV)**

John 13:19 "I am telling you now before it happens, so that when it does happen you will believe that I am who I am. **20** Very truly I tell you, whoever accepts anyone I send accepts me; and whoever accepts me accepts the one who sent me."

In other words, God, our Heavenly Father, would acknowledge all people who would come to be called Christians (aka Saved Gentiles) and the Jews who accepted Jesus as the Messiah, their Lord, and their Savior. Upon their death, God would usher them into Heaven.

REMEZ – Hidden Message

John 13:18 was a Remez for the following verses written by King David.

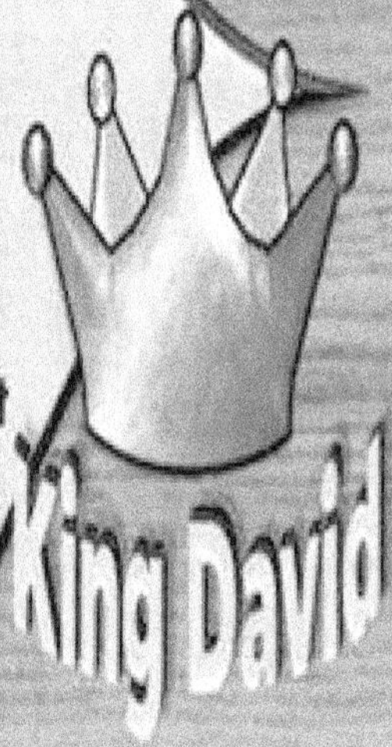

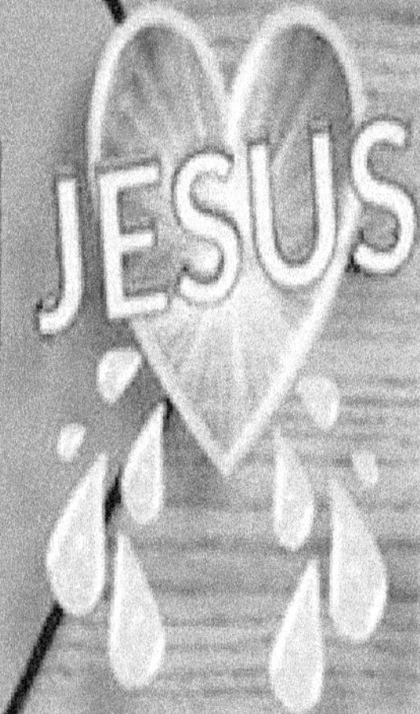

John 13:21 After he had said this, Jesus was troubled in spirit and testified, "Very truly I tell you, one of you is going to betray me." (NIV)

John 13:22 His disciples stared at one another, at a loss to know which of them he meant. (NIV)

John 13:23 One of them, the disciple whom Jesus loved, was reclining next to him. (NIV)

John 13:24 Simon Peter motioned to this disciple and said, "Ask him which one he means." (NIV)

John 13:25 Leaning back against Jesus, he asked him, "Lord, who is it?" (NIV)

John 13:26 Jesus answered, "It is the one to whom I will give this piece of bread when I have dipped it in the dish."

John 13:26B Then, dipping the piece of bread, he gave it to Judas, the son of Simon Iscariot.

John 13:27 As soon as Judas took the bread, Satan entered into him.

So Jesus told him, "What you are about to do, do quickly."

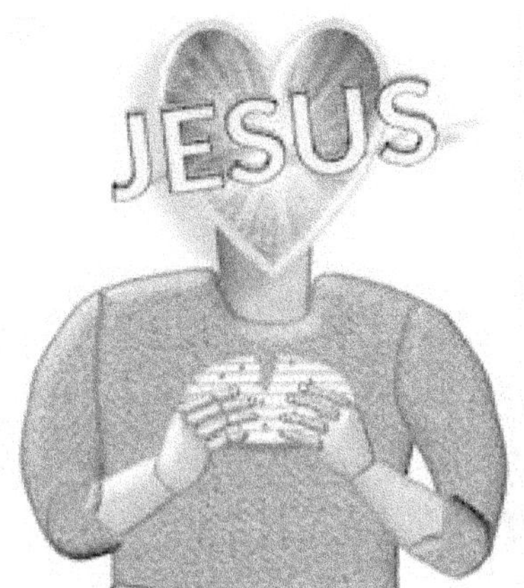

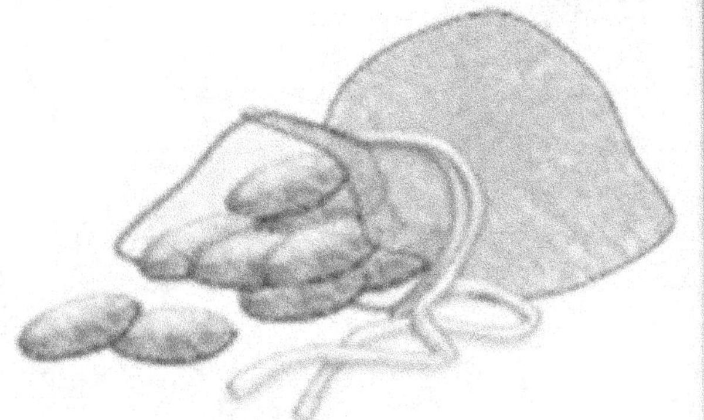

John 13:28 But no one at the meal understood why Jesus said this to him.

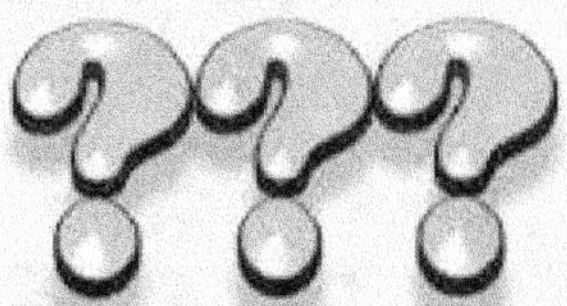

John 13:29 Since Judas had charge of the money, some thought Jesus was telling him to buy what was needed for the festival, or to give something to the poor. 30 As soon as Judas had taken the bread, he went out. And it was night. (NIV)

Last Supper Guest List:
Jesus
12 Disciples including Judas
Uninvited Guest - Devil
Only Jesus knew about the uninvited guest.

Which side of fence will you choose?
Not Now
Yes, Lord!

Throughout the day, we are bombarded with the options of which side of the fence we will choose.

We might be '*all in*' and say, "Yes, Lord, I proactively choose you and Your will for my life."

We might be undecided and say, "Not now." The challenge here is that we are not guaranteed to wake up in the morning. There is a significant risk in deferring your decision until later.

We might say an outright "No," which contains its potentially damaging challenges during our lifetime and after taking our last breath. **OR** we may strive to straddle the fence, trying to choose both sides at once.

It appears that Judas straddled the fence for three years. He vacillated between being a sincere Christ-follower and an insincere pretender, stealing money from the coffers and looking out for his self-interests rather than those of Jesus and his fellow Disciples.

Judas was not alone in having an **UNINVITED GUEST**. Satan has employed his minions to bombard us in such a way that we do not fulfill God's purpose for our lives.

If you are a student with a school assignment, an employee with job duties, a family member with a list of chores, a spouse with a '*Honey-do* list,' or, in my case, a writer with the goal to write a certain number of pages or chapters per day, one of his minions would be known as the **SPIRIT OF DISTRACTION** or **PROCRASTINATION**.

If you are a patient dealing with a diagnosis such as cancer, heart disease, kidney disease, diabetes, Parkinson's disease, etc., one of his minions would be known as the **SPIRIT OF DISCOURAGEMENT** or **HOPELESSNESS**.

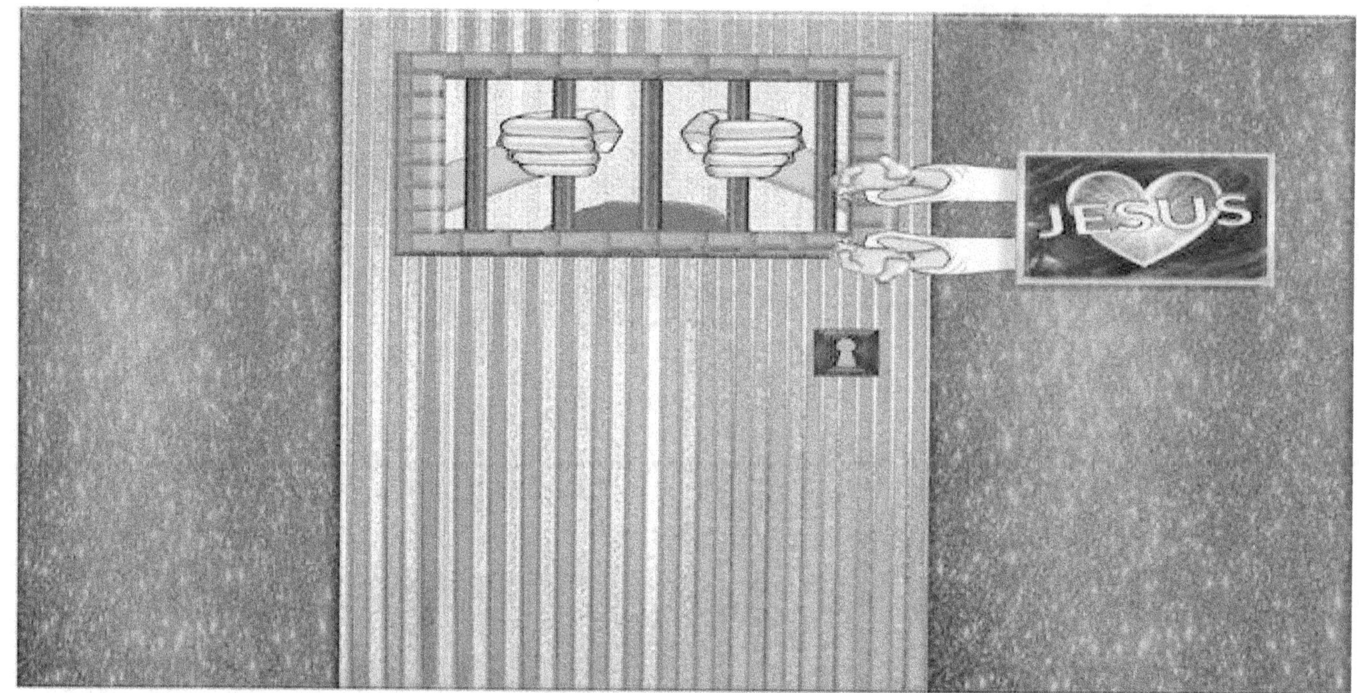

If you are an inmate of a jail, prison, or military camp or a child or teen who has been grounded, or a young person placed on probation, one of his minions would be known as the **SPIRIT OF BITTERNESS**, the **SPIRIT OF ANGER**, the **SPIRIT OF REVENGE**, or the **SPIRIT OF OUTRAGE** whispering words such as "No fair! They probably hate you!"

Those minions are doing their best to prevent you from feeling Jesus' love for you. They don't want you to hear His reassuring words, "You can still turn this around. I have confidence in you. Also, remember, I served time, too."

Another example is the spouse or partner dealing with being an abusive alcoholic.

Satan's minions may meet up with you after work. Perhaps they'll accompany you to the bar as you fortify yourself with a few drinks. Or maybe they'll lie in wait for you outside your abode so they can prod you to yell at, hit, or kick your spouse and/or kids.

Even though your spouse and kids can't physically see Satan's minions with their eyes, they can feel their presence. They know that you have not entered the house alone. Either knowingly or unknowingly, you have invited these minions to cheer you on as you implode inside and then explode with unfounded rage toward the people you claim to love.

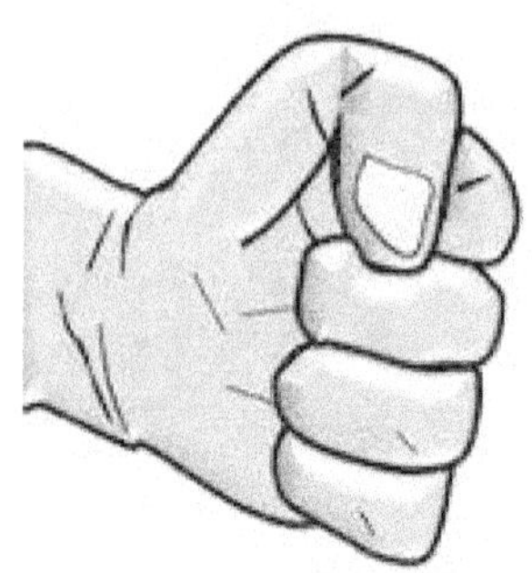

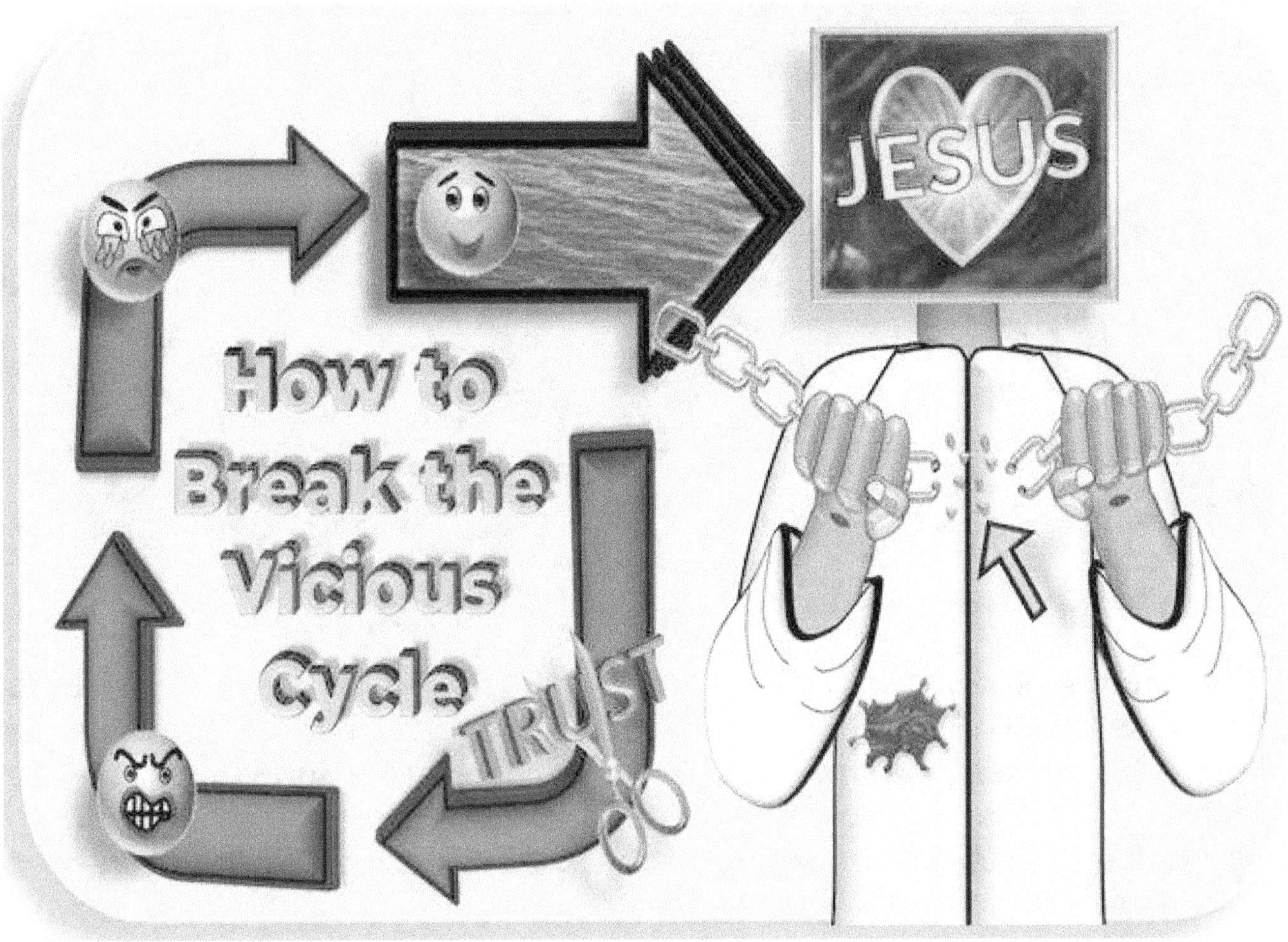

How to
Break the
Vicious
Cycle

JESUS

TRUST

Some habits are easier to break than others. The **POWER OF PRAYER** and **reading the Holy Bible** are an immense help. Some people find it helpful to find a support system such as counseling or plugging yourself into a twelve-step program such as Alcoholics Anonymous. In any case, Jesus also died on the cross for you to save you and to save your family. It's not too late to make the right choice.

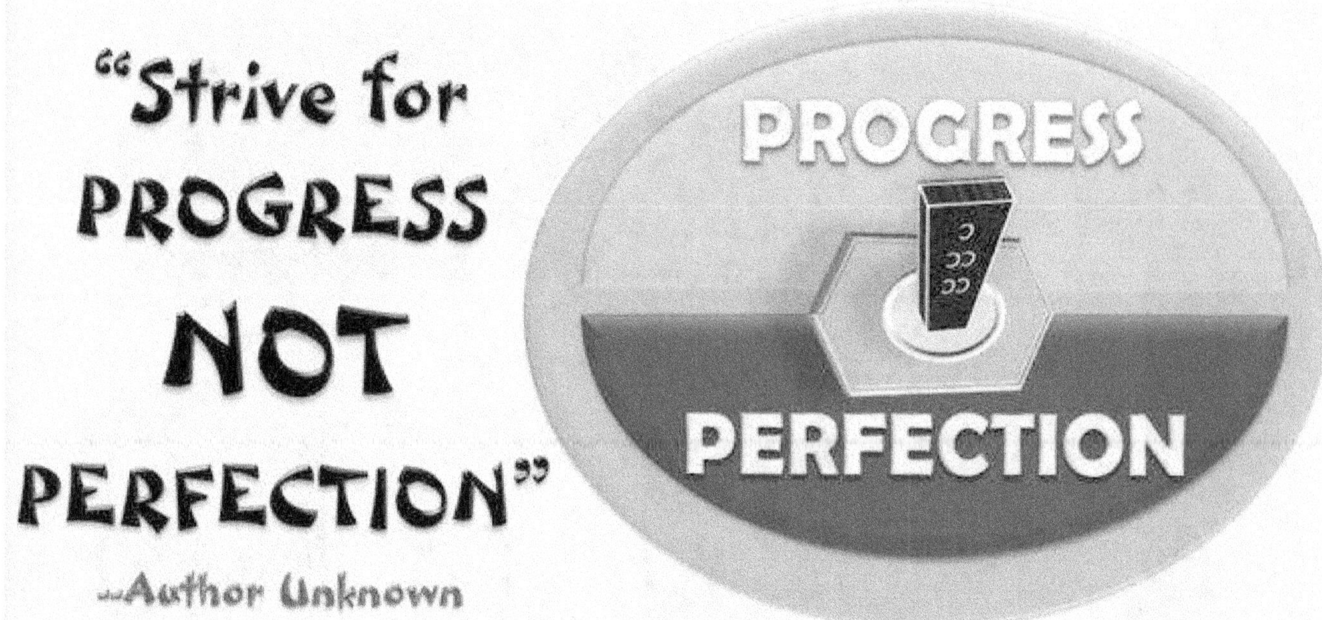

It might be helpful to focus on the words from this poster: "**Strive for Progress NOT Perfection.**" Only Jesus can be perfect. It would be impossible to compete with Him. We should also not try to compete with others. Instead, aim to do a little (or a lot) better than you previously did the day before. Jesus will judge our hearts. Just try to be the best version of yourself as possible, each and every day.

The Disciples were the first to receive the gift of the Holy Spirit after Jesus was crucified and resurrected. Since then, we who have repented of our sins and accepted Jesus as our Lord and Savior will forever have the Holy Spirit living inside us.

As we learn in **Isaiah 11**, one of the many benefits of these God-directed, God-sanctioned gifts is that the Holy Spirit, upon request, will protect us from Satan's minions. First, consider the words of the Lord's Prayer.

Our Father, who art in Heaven.
Hallowed be Thy name.
Thy kingdom come,
Thy will be done,
on Earth as it is in Heaven.
Give us this day our daily bread.

Forgive us our trespasses
as we forgive those
who trespass against us.
Lead us not into temptation.
but deliver us from evil.

For thine is the kingdom,
and the power,
and the glory forever.
Amen. **Matthew 6:9-15, Luke 11:2-4**

Next, consider some of the incredible attributes of the Holy Spirit.

Now imagine that one or more of Satan's minions, the **SPIRIT OF REVENGE** or **BITTERNESS**, attempt to ensnare, entrap, and entangle you. First, remind yourself of the reassurance of **1 Corinthians 10:13**:

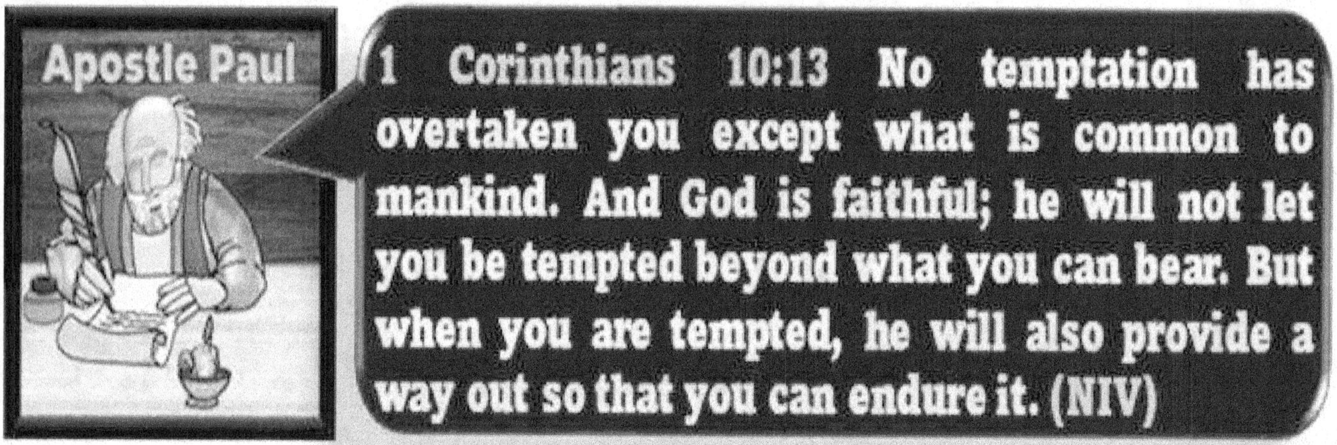

The way out is the Power of the Blood of Jesus that covers and protects us. We can pray something similar to this; however, feel free to use your own words that fit your comfort level in the way you pray.

Heavenly Father, Holy Spirit, King Jesus, in Jesus' Holy Name, I know you protect me from Satan and his minions with the Power of your Blood. Please route them out of my body, soul, and spirit. Afterward, fill all the vacated spaces with the power of the Holy Spirit. Thank you for being an ever-present help in every part of my life. Amen.

So much was at stake on that final night of Jesus' earthly life.

Satan's agenda was two-fold: (1) To encourage Judas to betray Jesus AND (2) Get the Sanhedrin to insist upon the death penalty for what they perceived as Jesus being a blasphemer. After all, Satan wanted Jesus to be dead, dead, dead, so that he and his minions could torture Him regularly.

Judas wanted to be able to keep those thirty pieces of silver given to him by the Jewish Temple Elders. Perhaps he hoped that they would employ him after he provided them with a way to circumvent the loyal followers of Jesus by arresting Him in an isolated place after dark. After all, he would no longer be the treasurer for Jesus and His Disciples. Perhaps he also entertained the idea that Jesus might finally be ready to employ His angels to neutralize the Romans when faced with the verdict of a brutal death.

The **Sanhedrin** eagerly waited for Judas to assist them in ridding Jerusalem of this troublesome pretender who claimed to be the Son of God.

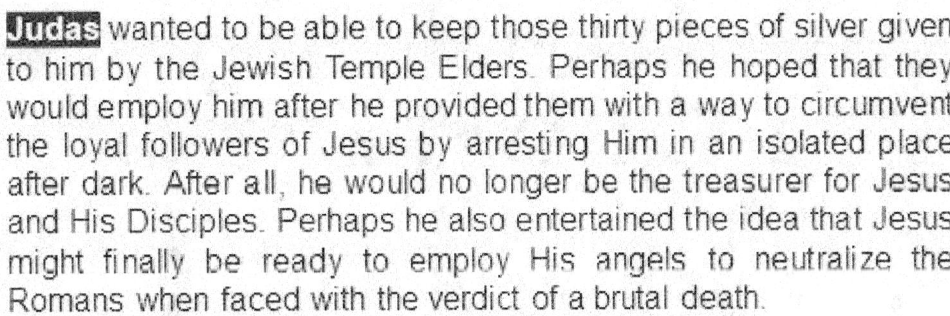

Jesus had that last evening to impart final words to His Disciples. He had already washed their feet. Next, Jesus planned to teach them about the practice of what is now called Holy Communion. He also had significant information to impart to His loyal eleven remaining Disciples less than twenty-four hours before His death.

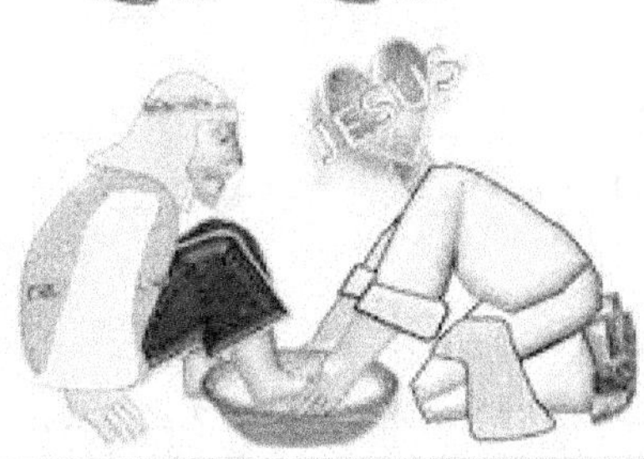

The eleven loyal **Disciples** of Jesus wanted to eat the Passover Seder with Jesus and each other. They also wanted to jockey for positions so that Jesus would choose one or only a few of them to be assigned titles of importance.

 I can almost picture them looking down from the clouds. Perhaps Archangel Michael and Archangel Gabriel paced back and forth in concern for what was to come. Did some of the Angels glance at each other in such a way to indicate that they would be ready to fly down to earth to assist Jesus should He call for them to do so? Was the Holy Spirit kept busy reminding Jesus of everything He was supposed to relay to the Disciples so the work of the Kingdom could continue? Was our Heavenly Father reminding Himself that for humanity to be Saved, He would have to turn His back on His beloved Son, Jesus? I can well imagine that more than one tear was being shed in Heaven. It's all I can do not to dissolve in tears myself as I picture that night and type these words.

What did Jesus and His twelve Disciples eat at their Last Supper? Sadly, there is extreme controversy about this very issue. Sigh! Double Sigh!

DISCLAIMER BY THE AUTHOR: *Once again, I exceedingly regret that, as a Gentile, I don't have a deeper understanding of Jewish holidays connected with Jesus. Before starting to write this book, the two things I knew were that:*

❶ *The Jewish Sabbath falls on Saturday. AND*

❷ *The annual spring holiday, the Passover Seder, had taken place ever since Pharoah finally released Moses and the Children of Israel about 1300 BC. This was after he and the Egyptians suffered the travails of ten plagues.*

As for Google, it is mostly my friend but sometimes my foe as I attempted to sift through the studies and conclusions posted by various Biblical scholars. I only wish that more of them would agree with each other so that I could feel like I am representing the Triune God as accurately as possible.

Also, be aware that the enemy <u>LOVES IT</u> that some of us get so caught up in arguing over relatively minor details that we sometimes don't advance God's kingdom as far as we could otherwise.

So, back to my original question, what did Jesus and His twelve Disciples eat at their Last Supper? We know for sure that there was Red Wine and platters of Unleavened Bread. However, I saw a smattering of Biblical scholars suggest leavened bread might have been present.

One of the most significant controversies among the Biblical scholars was whether they ate lamb at their Passover Seder meal.

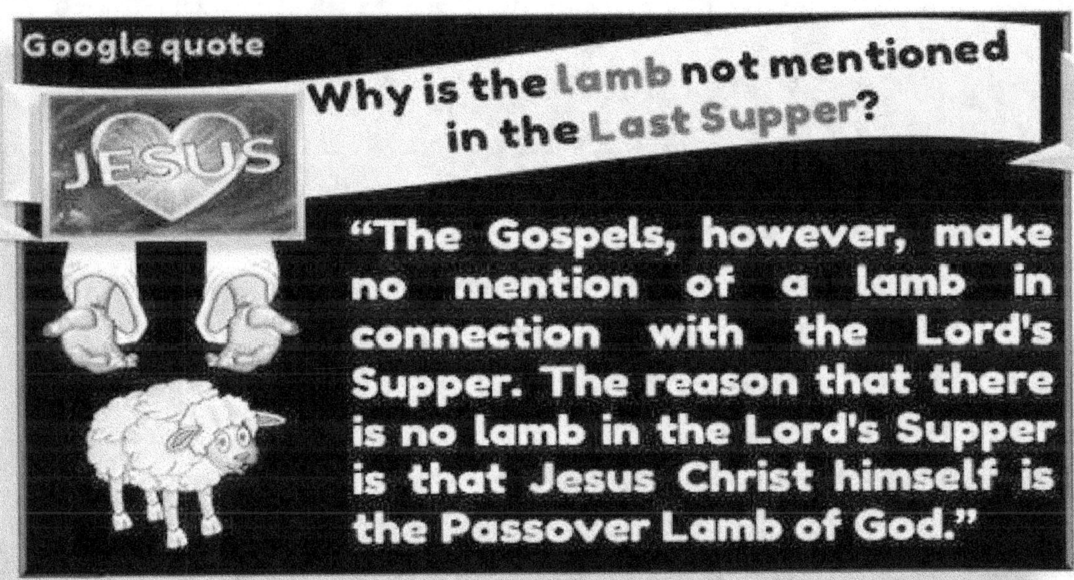

Pope Benedict XVI, who served the Catholic Church as the pope from 2005 to 2013, made the following statement.

"In the Cenacle [i.e., Upper Room where they ate their meal], Passover was probably celebrated without the lamb, says Benedict XVI, indicating that the calendar of the Qumran [i.e., part of the Dead Sea Scrolls] points to the exact moment of Christ's death. By laying down His life He gives true meaning to the ancient memorial of freedom from Egypt."

Since I learn best by writing and researching, let's examine the four Gospels for clues as to the best or most accurate answer.

Leviticus 23:4 "'These are the Lord's appointed festivals, the sacred assemblies you are to proclaim at their appointed times: 5 The Lord's Passover begins at twilight on the fourteenth day of the first month.

Leviticus 23:6 On the fifteenth day of that month the Lord's Festival of Unleavened Bread begins; for seven days you must eat bread made without yeast. 7 On the first day hold a sacred assembly and do no regular work. 8 For seven days present a food offering to the Lord. And on the seventh day hold a sacred assembly and do no regular work.'" (NIV)

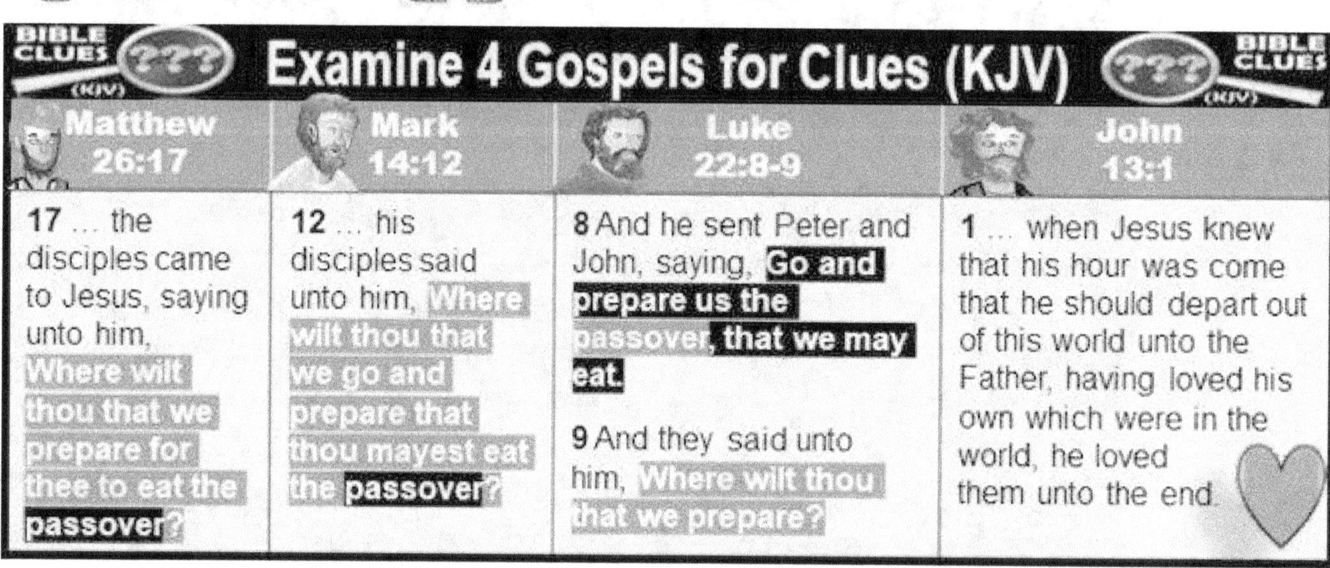

Examine 4 Gospels for Clues (KJV)

Matthew 26:18	Mark 14:13	Luke 22:10	John
18 And he said, Go into the city to such a man, ...	13 And he sendeth forth two of his disciples, and saith unto them, Go ye into the city, and there shall meet you a man bearing a pitcher of water: follow him.	10 And he said unto them, Behold, when ye are entered into the city, there shall a man meet you, bearing a pitcher of water; follow him into the house where he entereth in.	No Reference to this Topic.

Examine 4 Gospels for Clues (KJV)

Matthew 26:18	Mark 14:14	Luke 22:11	John
18 ... and say unto him, The Master saith, My time is at hand; I will keep the passover at thy house with my disciples.	14 And wheresoever he shall go in, say ye to the goodman of the house, The Master saith, Where is the guestchamber, where I shall eat the passover with my disciples?	11 And ye shall say unto the goodman of the house, The Master saith unto thee, Where is the guestchamber, where I shall eat the passover with my disciples?	No Reference to this Topic.

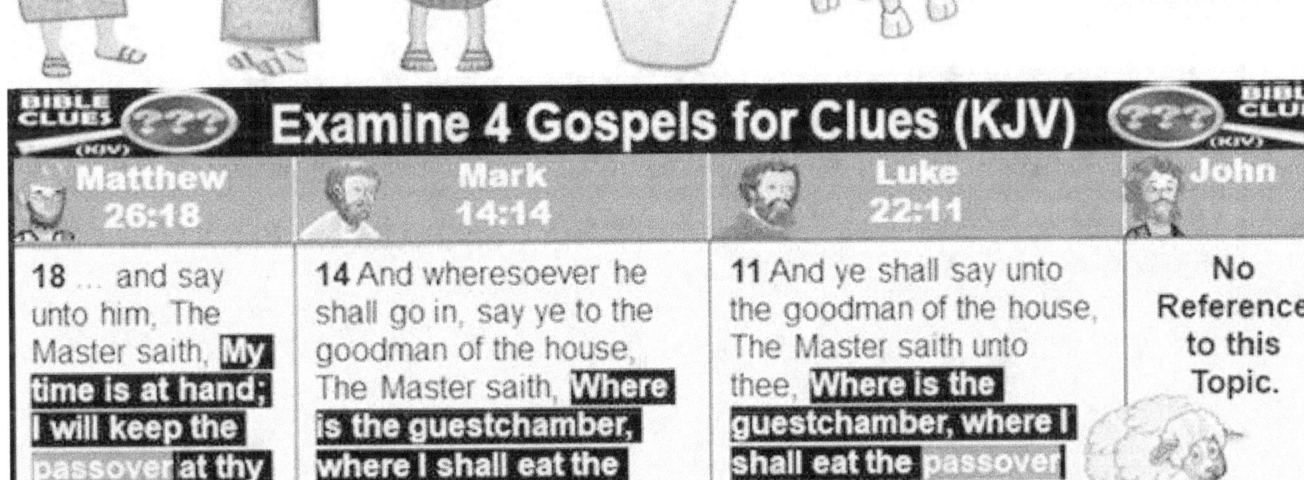

Examine 4 Gospels for Clues (KJV)

Matthew 26:19	Mark 14:15	Luke 22:12	John
19 And the disciples did as Jesus had appointed them; and they made ready the passover.	15 And he will shew you a large upper room furnished and prepared: there make ready for us.	12 And he shall shew you a large upper room furnished: there make ready.	No Reference to this Topic.

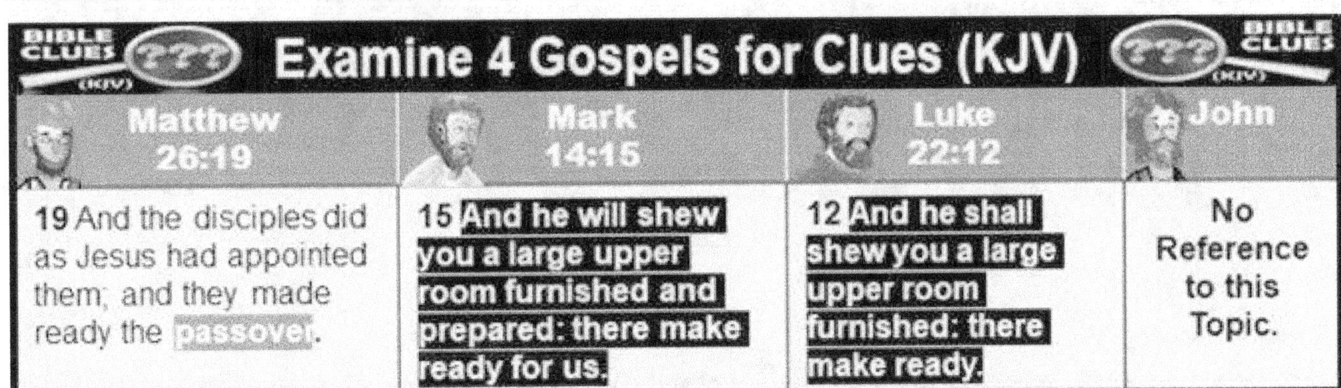

By cloaking the Last Supper's location in mystery, I concluded this clever plan must have been partly to prevent Judas from spoiling the Last Supper. Jesus knew that John and Peter would have to go to the holder of the money bags, Judas, to get funds to purchase Last Supper supplies. If Judas asked them, "Where will we eat the Passover Seder tonight?" - both Disciples could honestly say they had no clue. That way, nothing would stand in the way of Jesus having this final meal with His beloved Disciples.

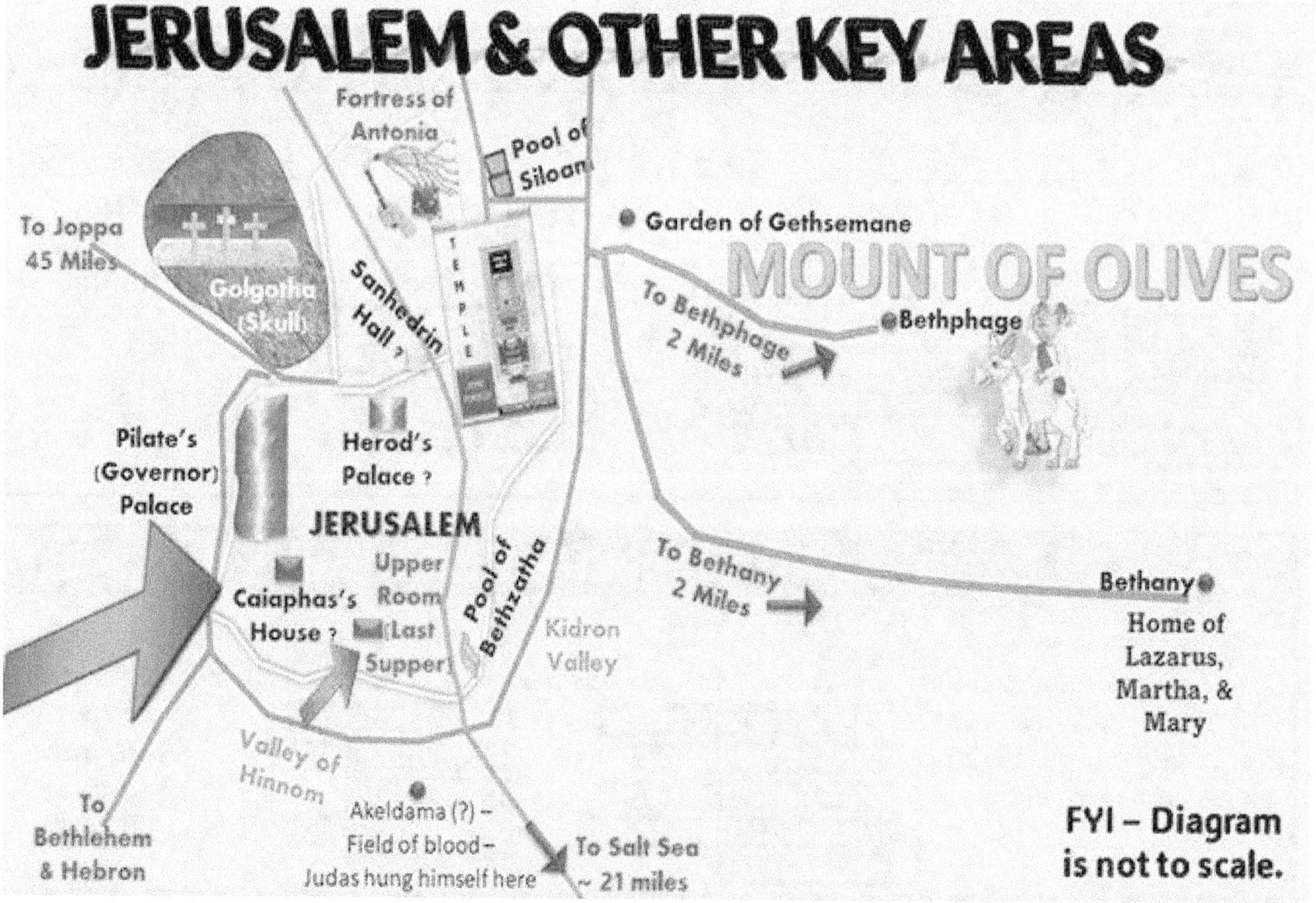

JERUSALEM & OTHER KEY AREAS

Matthew 26:19	Mark 14:16	Luke 22:13	John
19 And the disciples did as Jesus had appointed them; and they made ready the **passover**.	**16** And his disciples went forth, and came into the city, and found as he had said unto them: and they made ready the **passover**.	**13** And they went, and found as he had said unto them: and they made ready the **passover**.	**No Reference to this Topic.**

Matthew 26:20	Mark 14:17	Luke 22:14	John 13:1
20 Now when the even was come, he sat down with the twelve.	**17** And in the evening he cometh with the twelve.	**14** And when the hour was come, he sat down, and the twelve apostles with him.	**1** … when Jesus knew that his hour was come that he should depart out of this world unto the Father, having loved his own which were in the world, he loved them unto the end.

Matthew 26:26	Mark 14:22	Luke 22:19	John 6:1-71
26 And as they were eating, Jesus took bread, and blessed it, and brake it, and gave it to the disciples, and said, **Take, eat; this is my body.**	**22** And as they did eat, Jesus took bread, and blessed, and brake it, and gave to them, and said, **Take, eat: this is my body.**	**19** And he took bread, and gave thanks, and brake it, and gave unto them, saying, **This is my body which is given for you: this do in remembrance of me.**	John recounted, in **John 6:1-71**, about the shocking thing Jesus told his followers the day after He fed the 5,000. See upcoming details.

Unlike the Bible books of Matthew, Mark, and Luke, John does not tell the story of the Bread and Wine incident at the Last Supper. Instead, in the **sixth chapter of John**, he describes what happened a few days prior when 5000 hungry people sat on the side of a nearby mountain to listen to Jesus. Those people were equally eager to witness how He caused the lame to walk, the blind to see, the deaf to hear, and many sick people made well.

Well aware of the hungry people, Jesus asked the Disciples, in **John 6:5**, "**Where shall we buy bread for these people to eat?**"

Philip stated in **John 6:7**, "It would take more than half a year's wages to buy enough bread for each one to have a bite!" John noticed that Jesus looked more disappointed in Philip's lack of spiritual imagination than in his reply.

Jesus perked up a bit when Andrew came forward and said, in **John 6:9**, "Here is a boy with five small barley loaves and two small fish, but how far will they go among so many?" **(NIV)**

In **John 6:10**, Jesus said, "**Have the people sit down.**"

John 6:10 There was plenty of grass in that place, and they sat down (about five thousand men were there). 11 Jesus then took the loaves, gave thanks, and distributed to those who were seated as much as they wanted. He did the same with the fish.

John 6:12 When they had all had enough to eat, he said to his disciples, "Gather the pieces that are left over. Let nothing be wasted." 13 So they gathered them and filled twelve baskets with the pieces of the five barley loaves left over by those who had eaten.

John 6:14 After the people saw the sign Jesus performed, they began to say, "Surely this is the Prophet who is to come into the world." 15 Jesus, knowing that they intended to come and make him king by force, withdrew again to a mountain by himself. (NIV)

The next day, the people searched for Jesus for a repeat performance. They finally found him when they reached Capernaum on the lake's opposite shore. In **John 6:25**, they asked Him, "Rabbi, when did you get here?"

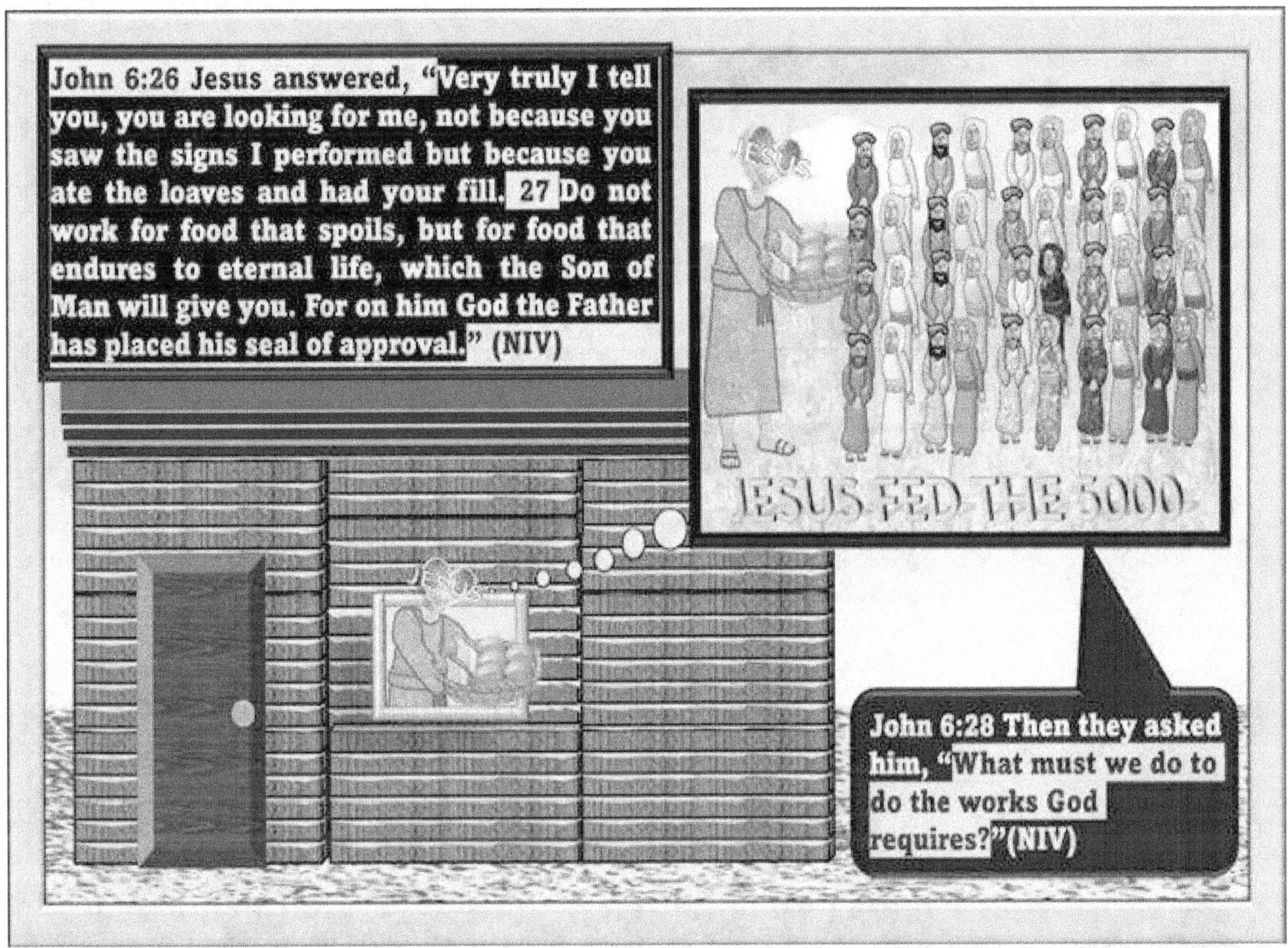

John 6:29 Jesus answered, "The work of God is this: to believe in the one he has sent."

John 6:30 So they asked him, "What sign then will you give that we may see it and believe you? What will you do? 31 Our ancestors ate the manna in the wilderness; as it is written: 'He gave them bread from heaven to eat.'"

God

John 6:32 Jesus said to them, "Very truly I tell you, it is not Moses who has given you the bread from heaven, but it is my Father who gives you the true bread from heaven. 33 For the bread of God is the bread that comes down from heaven and gives life to the world."

John 6:34 "Sir," they said, "always give us this bread.**" (NIV)**

Up to that point, the people were pleased with Jesus. But what He said next shocked and confused them so much that many ceased to follow after Him.

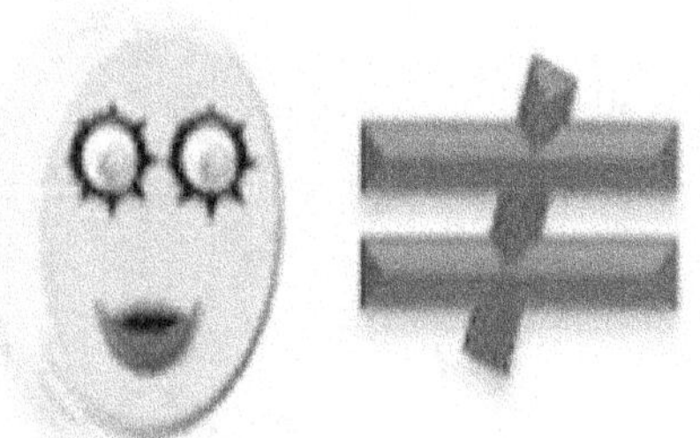
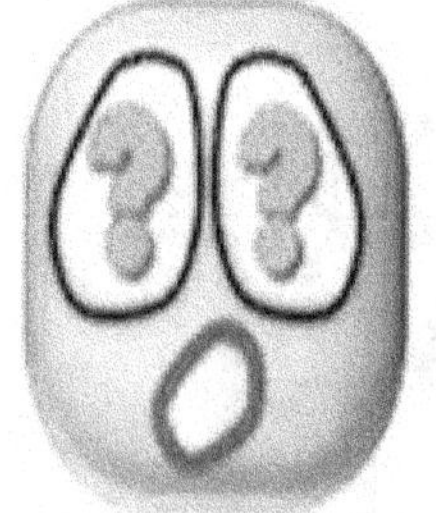

John 6:35 Then Jesus declared, "I am the bread of life. Whoever comes to me will never go hungry, and whoever believes in me will never be thirsty. 36 But as I told you, you have seen me and still you do not believe. 37 All those the Father gives me will come to me, and whoever comes to me I will never drive away." (NIV)

John 6:38 "For I have come down from heaven not to do my will but to do the will of him who sent me. 39 And this is the will of him who sent me, that I shall lose none of all those he has given me, but raise them up at the last day. 40 For my Father's will is that everyone who looks to the Son and believes in him shall have eternal life, and I will raise them up at the last day." (NIV)

John 6:41 At this the Jews there began to grumble about him because he said, "I am the bread that came down from heaven." 42 They said, "Is this not Jesus, the son of Joseph, whose father and mother we know? How can he now say, 'I came down from heaven'?" (NIV)

John 6:43 "Stop grumbling among yourselves," Jesus answered.

John 6:44 "No one can come to me unless the Father who sent me draws them, and I will raise them up at the last day.

John 6:45 It is written in the Prophets: 'They will all be taught by God.' Everyone who has heard the Father and learned from him comes to me. 46 No one has seen the Father except the one who is from God; only he has seen the Father. 47 Very truly I tell you, the one who believes has eternal life. (NIV)

REMEZ
Hidden Messages

Isaiah 54:13 All your children will be taught by the Lord, and great will be their peace. (NIV)

REMEZ
Hidden Messages

Jeremiah 31:33 "This is the covenant I will make with the people of Israel after that time," declares the Lord. "I will put my law in their minds and write it on their hearts. I will be their God, and they will be my people." (NIV)

Jeremiah 31:34 "No longer will they teach their neighbor, or say to one another, 'Know the Lord,' because they will all know me, from the least of them to the greatest," declares the Lord. "For I will forgive their wickedness and will remember their sins no more." (NIV)

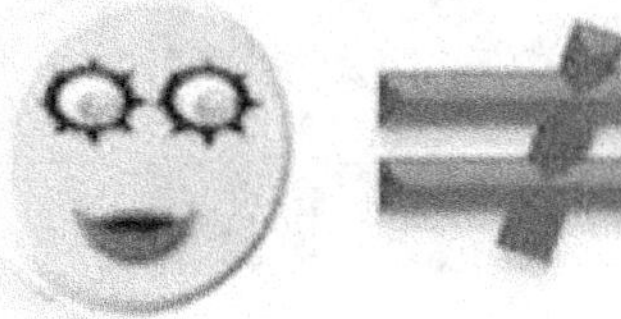

Psalm 32:8 I will instruct you and teach you in the way you should go; I will counsel you with my loving eye on you. (NIV)

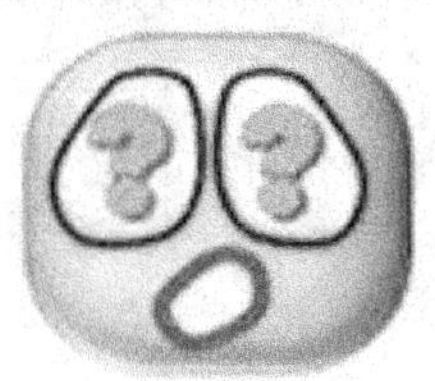

If those words weren't challenging enough for His followers to accept, His subsequent words caused many of His Followers to desert Him. Perhaps Jesus was drawing a line in the sand. He could have explained that His next words were symbolic rather than to be taken literally. Jesus certainly was not suggesting that they suddenly transform into cannibals who would kill, cook, and then eat His flesh. It might have been Jesus' way of separating the wheat from the chaff. Got Questions.org explains it in this way.

"To prevent being misconstrued, Jesus specifies that He has been speaking metaphorically: "The Spirit gives life; the flesh counts for nothing. The words I have spoken to you—they are full of the Spirit and life" (John 6:63). Those who misunderstood Jesus and were offended by His talk about eating His flesh and drinking His blood were stuck in a physical mindset, ignoring the things of the Spirit. They were concerned with getting another physical meal, so Jesus uses the realm of the physical to teach a vital spiritual truth. Those who couldn't make the jump from the physical to the spiritual turned their backs on Jesus and walked away (verse 66)."

"At the Last Supper, Jesus gives a similar message and one that complements His words in John 6—when the disciples gather to break bread and drink the cup, they "proclaim the Lord's death until he comes" (1 Corinthians 11:26). In fact, Jesus said that the bread broken at the table is His body, and the cup they drink is the new covenant in His blood, shed for the forgiveness of sins (Matthew 26:26–28). Their act of eating and drinking was to be a symbol of their faith in Christ. Just as physical food gives earthly life, Christ's sacrifice on the cross gives heavenly life."

John 6:48 "I am the bread of life. 49 Your ancestors ate the manna in the wilderness, yet they died. 50 But here is the bread that comes down from heaven, which anyone may eat and not die.

John 6:51 I am the living bread that came down from heaven. Whoever eats this bread will live forever. This bread is my flesh, which I will give for the life of the world." (NIV)

John 6:52 Then the Jews began to argue sharply among themselves, "How can this man give us his flesh to eat?" (NIV)

John 6:53 Jesus said to them, "Very truly I tell you, unless you eat the flesh of the Son of Man and drink his blood, you have no life in you. 54 Whoever eats my flesh and drinks my blood has eternal life, and I will raise them up at the last day. 55 For my flesh is real food and my blood is real drink. 56 Whoever eats my flesh and drinks my blood remains in me, and I in them.

John 6:57 Just as the living Father sent me and I live because of the Father, so the one who feeds on me will live because of me. 58 This is the bread that came down from heaven. Your ancestors ate manna and died, but whoever feeds on this bread will live forever." (NIV)

John 6:59 He said this while teaching in the synagogue in Capernaum.

John 6:60 On hearing it, many of his disciples said, "This is a hard teaching. Who can accept it?" (NIV)

John 6:61 Aware that his disciples were grumbling about this, Jesus said to them, "Does this offend you? 62 Then what if you see the Son of Man ascend to where he was before! 63 The Spirit gives life; the flesh counts for nothing. The words I have spoken to you—they are full of the Spirit and life."(NIV)

John 6:64 "Yet there are some of you who do not believe." For Jesus had known from the beginning which of them did not believe and who would betray him. 65 He went on to say, "This is why I told you that no one can come to me unless the Father has enabled them." (NIV)

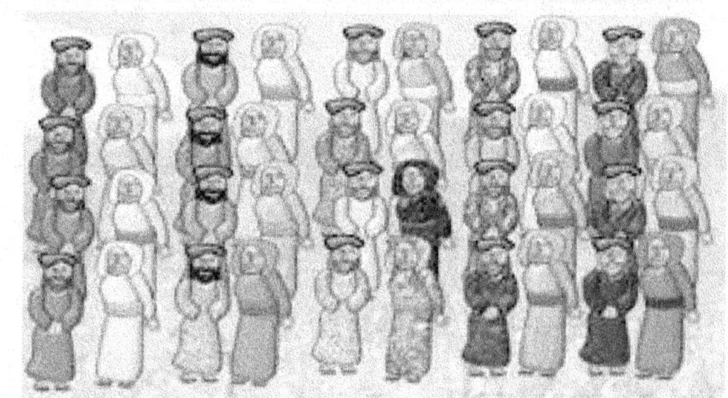

John 6:66 From this time many of his disciples turned back and no longer followed him. (NIV)

John 6:67 "You do not want to leave too, do you?" Jesus asked the Twelve. (NIV)

We can imagine this must have been a very challenging moment for Jesus. It is never fun or easy to be misunderstood or deserted by people who claim to be your friends or followers.

John 6:68 Simon Peter answered him, "Lord, to whom shall we go? You have the words of eternal life. 69 We have come to believe and to know that you are the Holy One of God." (NIV)

John 6:70 Then Jesus replied, "Have I not chosen you, the Twelve? Yet one of you is a devil!" 71 (He meant Judas, the son of Simon Iscariot, who, though one of the Twelve, was later to betray him.) (NIV)

Judas
Iscariot

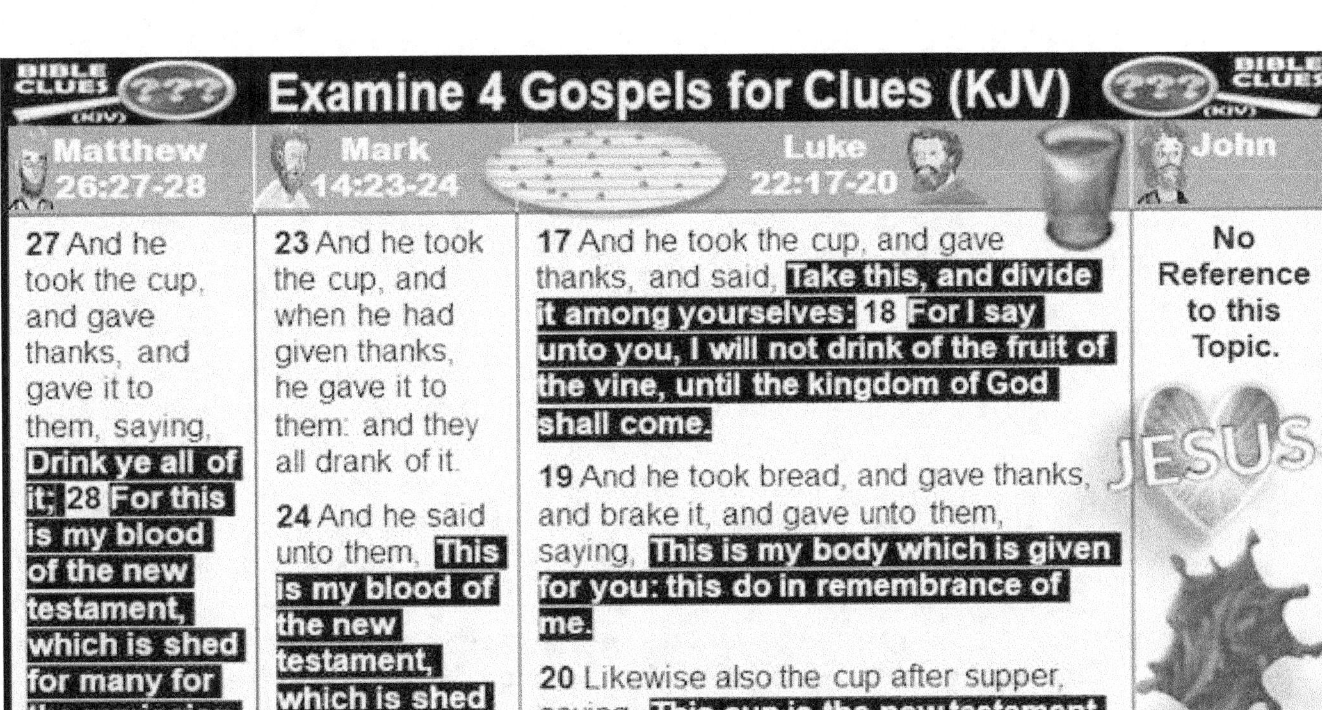

BIBLE CLUES ??? (KJV)

Examine 4 Gospels for Clues (KJV)

??? BIBLE CLUES (KJV)

Matthew 26:27-28

Mark 14:23-24

Luke 22:17-20

John

27 And he took the cup, and gave thanks, and gave it to them, saying, Drink ye all of it; 28 For this is my blood of the new testament, which is shed for many for the remission of sins.

23 And he took the cup, and when he had given thanks, he gave it to them: and they all drank of it.

24 And he said unto them, This is my blood of the new testament, which is shed for many.

17 And he took the cup, and gave thanks, and said, Take this, and divide it among yourselves: 18 For I say unto you, I will not drink of the fruit of the vine, until the kingdom of God shall come.

19 And he took bread, and gave thanks, and brake it, and gave unto them, saying, This is my body which is given for you: this do in remembrance of me.

20 Likewise also the cup after supper, saying, This cup is the new testament in my blood, which is shed for you.

No Reference to this Topic.

JESUS

BIBLE CLUES ??? (KJV)

Examine 4 Gospels for Clues (KJV)

??? BIBLE CLUES (KJV)

Matthew 26:29

Unleavened Bread

Mark 14:25

Luke 22:15-16

John

29 But I say unto you, I will not drink henceforth of this fruit of the vine, until that day when I drink it new with you in my Father's kingdom.

25 Verily I say unto you, I will drink no more of the fruit of the vine, until that day that I drink it new in the kingdom of God.

15 And he said unto them, With desire I have desired to eat this passover with you before I suffer: 16 For I say unto you, I will not any more eat thereof, until it be fulfilled in the kingdom of God.

No Reference to this Topic.

JESUS

1 Upper Room

2 Reclining at Table

3 Awareness of final hours

4 Jesus washed their feet

5 Reveal Judas' Betrayal

Agenda for the Last Supper

6 Bread and Wine

7 Short time left revealed

8 Peter will deny Him 3 times

9 Who is the greatest Disciple?

10 Upcoming Spiritual Warfare

As the Last Supper continued, Jesus was hyper-aware of what a short time He had to try to convey a boatload of information. I'm sure He took comfort in knowing that after His crucifixion, resurrection, and ascension to Heaven, He could send them the ultimate comforter, the Holy Spirit. The Holy Spirit would equip them to fully recall and comprehend all His former teachings.

John 13:31 Therefore, when he [i.e., Judas Iscariot] was gone out, Jesus said, Now is the Son of man glorified, and God is glorified in him. **32** If God be glorified in him, God shall also glorify him in himself, and shall straightway glorify him.

John 13:33 Little children, yet a little while I am with you. Ye shall seek me: and as I said unto the Jews, Whither I go, ye cannot come; so now I say to you.

John 13:34 A new commandment I give unto you, That ye love one another; as I have loved you, that ye also love one another. **35** By this shall all men know that ye are my disciples, if ye have love one to another. **(NIV)**

All four Gospels tell the story of one of the final interactions between Peter and Jesus at the Last Supper.

First, Jesus made the Remez statement that hearkens back to **Zechariah 13:7**. We learn that Jesus said:

> **Matthew 26:31 & Mark 14:27 "All ye shall be offended because of me this night: for it is written, I will smite the shepherd, and the sheep of the flock shall be scattered abroad." (KJV)**

Looking ahead, later that evening, after Jesus was arrested in the Garden of Gethsemane, all of His faithful Disciples scattered and went into hiding in fear for their lives. Ironically, just a few hours before, they all had echoed Peter in stating that such a thing could never happen.

Similarly, Zechariah describes this concept in this way: **Zechariah 13:7** Awake, O sword, against my shepherd, and against the man that is my fellow, saith the Lord of hosts: smite the shepherd, and the sheep shall be scattered: and I will turn mine hand upon the little ones.

Jesus knew that although they would scatter, they would all, minus Judas Iscariot, of course, soon reunite. Jesus instructed them:

> **Matthew 26:32 & Mark 14:28 "But after I am risen again, I will go before you into Galilee." (KJV)**

Peter, the Disciple with a big heart but a hasty tongue, valiantly declared:

Disciple
Peter

We learn some extra details about this prediction in **Luke 22:31**. Jesus stated, "Simon, Simon, behold, Satan hath desired to have you, that he may sift you as wheat." Observe that Jesus called him by his original name of Simon rather than his formerly earned title of Peter. Jesus continued, in **Luke 22:32**, "But I have prayed for thee, that thy faith fail not: and when thou art converted, strengthen thy brethren." (KJV)

Disciple
Peter

Simon Peter likely felt embarrassed and chagrined to hear such words from this master whom he had faithfully followed for the last three years. Perhaps without thinking it through or believing his own false bravado, he bravely defended himself by affirming, in **Luke 22:33**, "Lord, I am ready to go with thee, both into prison, and to death."

We can imagine a sad but loving smile appearing upon Jesus' face as he predicted, from **Matthew 26:34**, **Mark 14:30**, **Luke 22:34**, and **John 13:38**, "I tell thee, Peter, the cock shall not crow this day, before that thou shalt thrice deny that thou knowest me." (KJV)

In **Matthew 26:35** and **Mark 14:31**, we learn, "**But he (i.e., Simon Peter) spake the more vehemently,** If I should die with thee, I will not deny thee in any wise. **Likewise also said they all.**" (KJV)

One of Jesus' very subtle predictions went over the heads of every Disciple in that room. They would not understand this statement until years later as every one of them, except Disciple John, who survived until old age took him, would be martyred for their faith.

Disciple
Peter

By this, Jesus meant that just like the Roman soldiers would crucify Him the following day, in 64 AD, Peter would also be crucified.

So, when Peter replied to Jesus with a promissory statement in **John 13:37**, it would indeed be fulfilled not that night or the next day but about thirty years later. For "**Peter said unto him,** Lord, why cannot I follow thee now? I will lay down my life for thy sake." In retrospect, we understand that Peter did not have the courage to stand behind that promise under his own will and power. But once he was saved and filled with the **power of the Holy Spirit**, he could courageously and valiantly make his former prediction and promise come true. In those latter years, Peter could proudly live up to his adopted name of Peter, which in Greek and Latin meant Rock or Stone. Through the grace given Him by the **Triune God**, he could face this martyred death without fear.

Jesus graciously allowed the subject to drop as He had more ground to cover before they left the Upper Room.

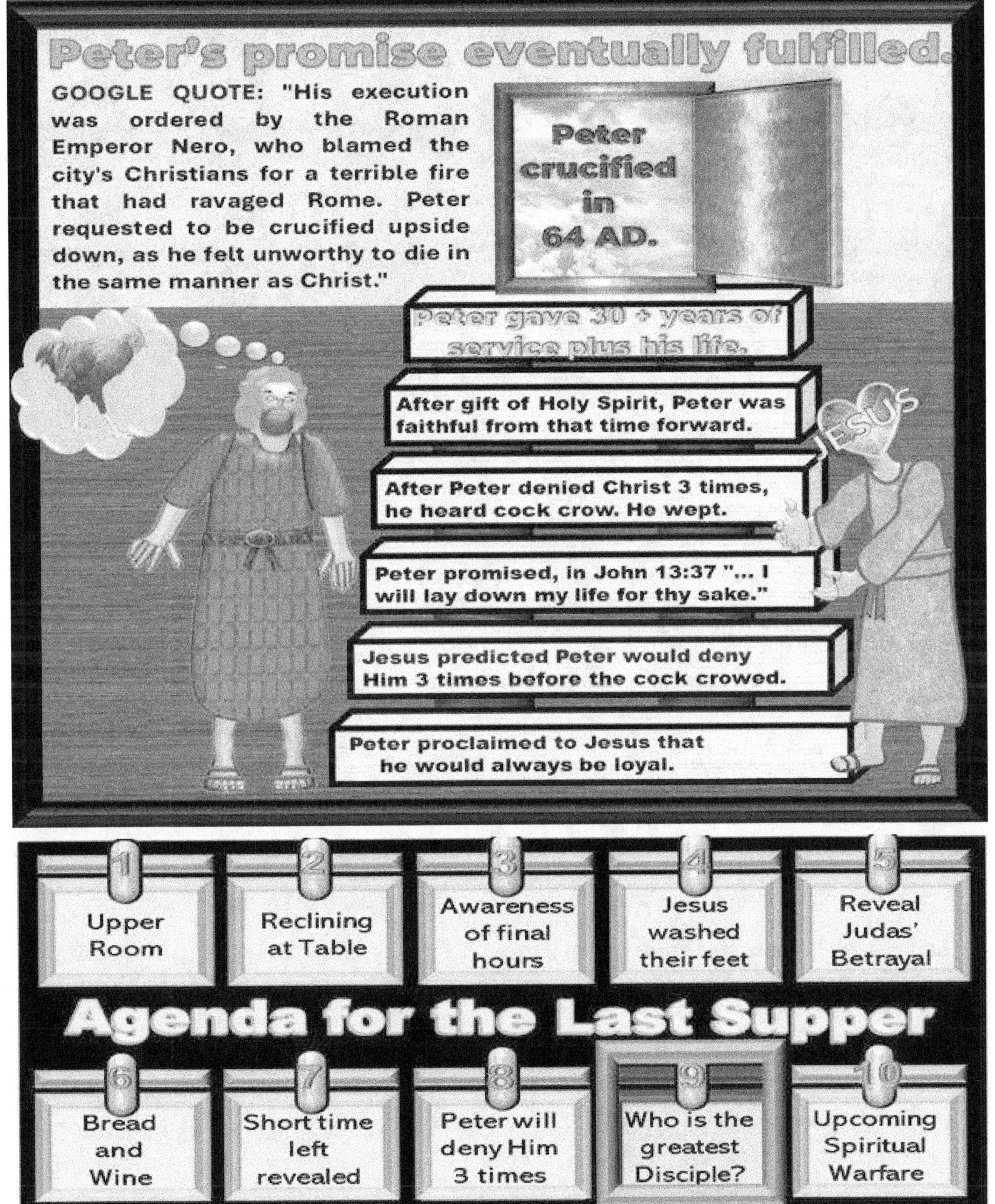

In **Luke 22:24-30**, the eleven remaining Disciples argued among themselves. What was their argument about? They wanted to determine which one of them was the greatest Disciple.

Jesus could see that His Disciples were still trying to box Him into their view of what a Messiah should be. They also were vying for a key role in their vision of Jesus suddenly transforming into King David at His warrior-best. So, Judas Iscariot was not alone in misinterpreting the true mission of Jesus, the only begotten Son of God most high when He incarnated onto the planet His Father created. In **Luke 22:25-30**, Jesus tried to get them to comprehend.

Luke 22:25 And he said unto them, The kings of the Gentiles exercise lordship over them; and they that exercise authority upon them are called benefactors. **(KJV)**

Luke 22:26 But ye shall not be so: but he that is greatest among you, let him be as the younger; and he that is chief, as he that doth serve. **(KJV)**

Luke 22:27 For whether is greater, he that sitteth at meat, or he that serveth? is not he that sitteth at meat? but I am among you as he that serveth. **(KJV)**

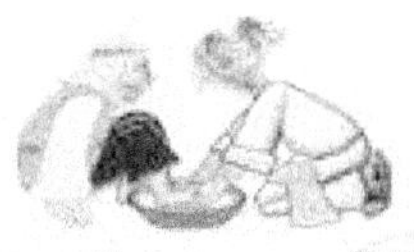

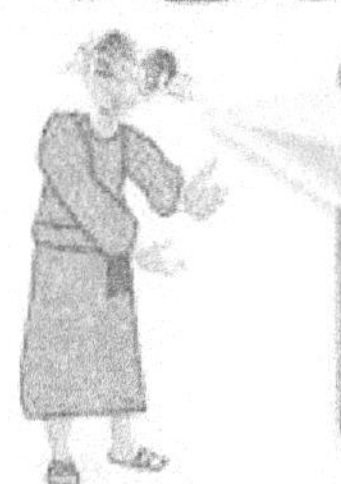

Jesus probably hoped they recalled that He had washed the feet of each one of them that very evening.

Luke 22:28 Ye are they which have continued with me in my temptations. (KJV)

Luke 22:29 And I appoint unto you a kingdom, as my Father hath appointed unto me; 30 That ye may eat and drink at my table in my kingdom, and sit on thrones judging the twelve tribes of Israel.

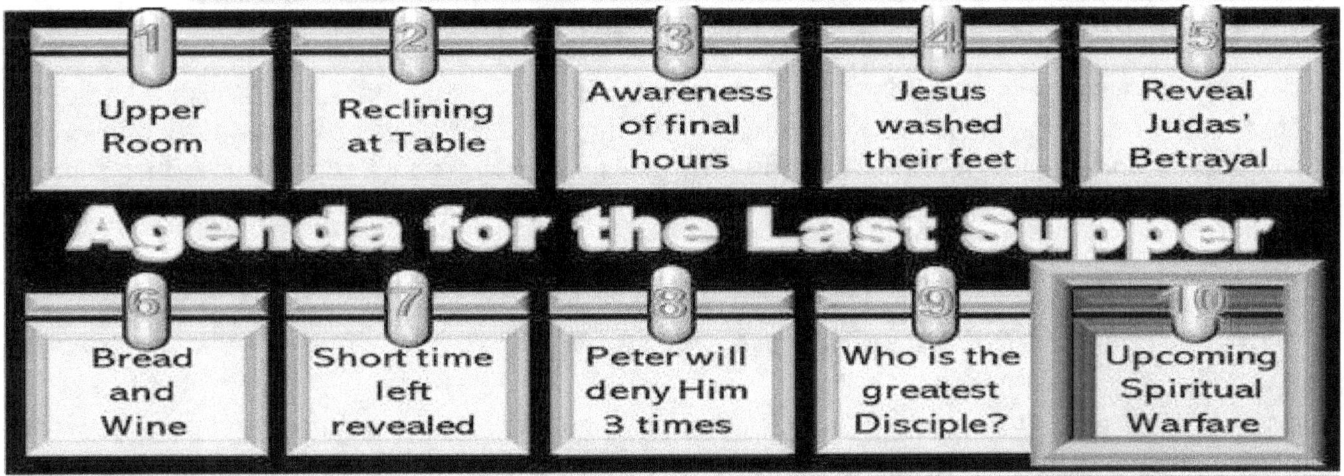
1
Upper Room
2
Reclining at Table
3
Awareness of final hours
4
Jesus washed their feet
5
Reveal Judas' Betrayal
Agenda for the Last Supper
6
Bread and Wine
7
Short time left revealed
8
Peter will deny Him 3 times
9
Who is the greatest Disciple?
10
Upcoming Spiritual Warfare

Jesus sent His Disciples, two-by-two, on a Mission trip of Healing

Mark 6:7 And he called the twelve and began to send them out two by two, and gave them authority over the unclean spirits. 8 He charged them to take nothing for their journey except a staff—no bread, no bag, no money in their belts — 9 but to wear sandals and not put on two tunics. (KJV)

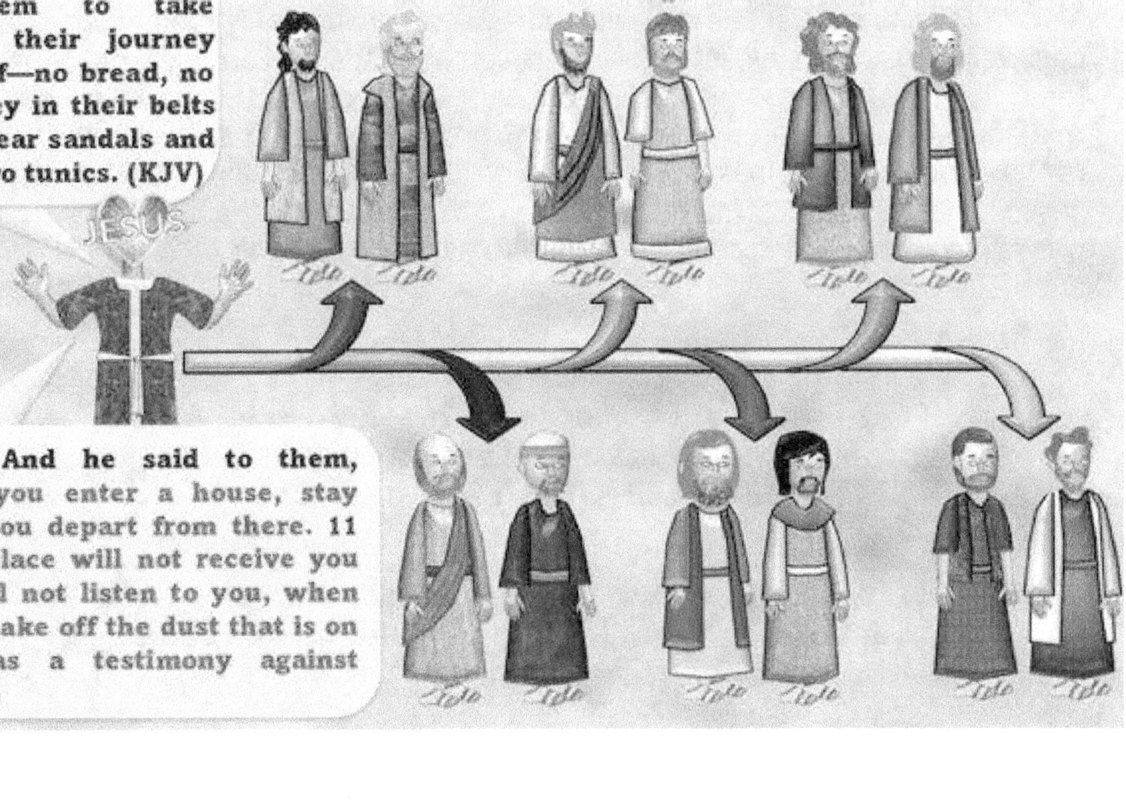
JESUS

Mark 6:10 And he said to them, "Whenever you enter a house, stay there until you depart from there. 11 And if any place will not receive you and they will not listen to you, when you leave, shake off the dust that is on your feet as a testimony against them." (KJV)

During the Last Supper, as often happens at get-togethers of family and friends, you find yourself reminiscing about former times.

In the same way, Jesus reminded them of what happened to them earlier in His ministry. He had sent off his twelve Disciples and some of His faithful followers to minister to people in various cities. The group of 70 traveled two-by-two. This incident was described in **Mark 6:7-13**, **Matthew 10:1-42**, **Luke 9:1-6**, and **Luke 10:1-22**.

At that time, because people were excited by Jesus' novel teachings, His charitable practices, and all the healings He provided, that group of 70 people was treated with great hospitality. The Disciples and followers were greatly exhilarated as they returned from their journey to report to Jesus.

Jesus knew He had to prepare His Disciples for what was to come. Where before they were mostly welcomed with open arms, now they would be viewed with great hostility. So, Jesus said:

Many a Biblical scholar has speculated if Jesus was suddenly promoting violence instead of passively 'turning the other cheek.' Of course, swords can be used like an ax to cut wood, like a flint to create a spark to start a cooking fire, or as a self-defense weapon to ward off wild animal attacks and perhaps a bandit or two. Instead of taking the Bible verses out of context, focus on the messages preached during His ministry. If so, you will conclude that Jesus spoke of swords symbolically rather than in reality. In the short time He had left, Jesus was trying to prepare His disciples to be vigilant about facing up to **SPIRITUAL WARFARE** of various types.

When Peter and probably the other Simon, Simon the Zealot, pulled out their swords, Jesus probably groaned on the inside. When He responded, "It is enough," He probably meant "Enough of this. I'm just wasting my words." Meanwhile, the Disciples likely concluded, "Oh, good. Jesus approves of us having two swords."

As a 7th-grade member of the Prayer Club in my junior high (1970-71), I still remember our club members listening to the 1969 soundtrack of 'Jesus Christ Superstar.' In despair, the man who played Jesus sang, "Look at your blank faces. My life will mean nothing – ten minutes after I'm dead." The actual Jesus might have begun to feel greatly discouraged, inwardly questioning whether His Disciples would ever grasp the lessons He had tried so hard to teach them. That must have been a challenging moment indeed.

Luke 22:37 For I say unto you, that this that is written must yet be accomplished in me, And he was reckoned among the transgressors: for the things concerning me have an end. **(KJV)**

REMEZ Hidden Messages

Isaiah 53:12 "Therefore will I divide him a portion with the great, and he shall divide the spoil with the strong; because he hath poured out his soul unto death: and he was numbered with the transgressors; and he bare the sin of many, and made intercession for the transgressors." **(KJV)**

In, **John 14 to 16,** we learn from Disciple John that Jesus had much more to convey regarding **SPIRITUAL WARFARE**. By looking at the **NIV Bible** as seen on Bible Gateway.com, John divides these points into seven sections:

(1) **(1) The World Hates the Disciples (John 15:18-25) [Synopsis of key verses]**

John 15:18 If the world hate you, ye know that it hated me before it hated you. **(KJV)**

John 15:20 ... If they have persecuted me, they will also persecute you. ... **(KJV)**

John 15:23 He that hateth me hateth my Father also. **(KJV)**

John 15:24 If I had not done among them the works which none other man did, they had not had sin: but now have they both seen and hated both me and my Father. (KJV)

John 15:25 But this cometh to pass, that the word might be fulfilled that is written in their law, They hated me without a cause. (KJV)

Psalm 69:4 They that hate me without a cause are more than the hairs of mine head: they that would destroy me, being mine enemies wrongfully, are mighty: then I restored that which I took not away. (KJV)

(2) Jesus Comforts His Disciples (John 14:1-4)

John 14:1 Let not your heart be troubled: ye believe in God, believe also in me. (KJV)

John 14:2 In my Father's house are many mansions: if it were not so, I would have told you. I go to prepare a place for you. (KJV)

John 14:3 And if I go and prepare a place for you, I will come again, and receive you unto myself; that where I am, there ye may be also. (KJV)

John 14:4 And whither I go ye know, and the way ye know. (KJV)

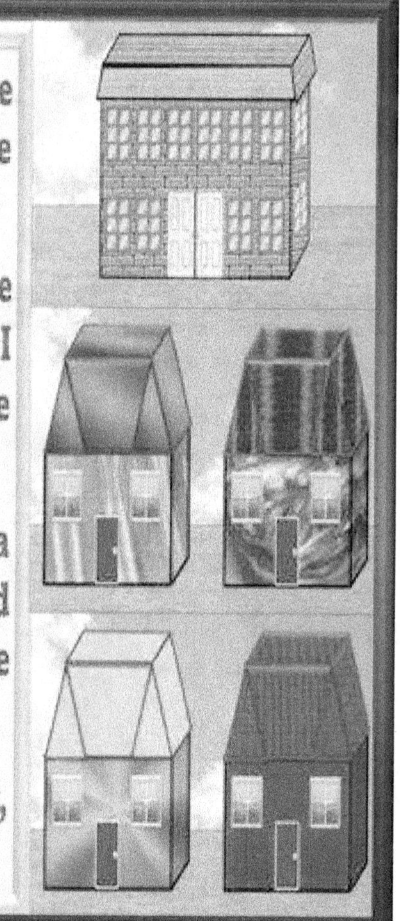

John 14:5 Thomas saith unto him, Lord, we know not whither thou goest; and how can we know the way? (KJV)

John 14:6 Jesus saith unto him, I am the way, the truth, and the life: no man cometh unto the Father, but by me.

John 14:7 If ye had known me, ye should have known my Father also: and from henceforth ye know him, and have seen him. (KJV)

John 14:8 Philip saith unto him, Lord, show us the Father, and it sufficeth us. (KJV)

John 14:9 Jesus saith unto him, Have I been so long time with you, and yet hast thou not known me, Philip? he that hath seen me hath seen the Father; and how sayest thou then, Show us the Father?

John 14:10 Believest thou not that I am in the Father, and the Father in me? the words that I speak unto you I speak not of myself: but the Father that dwelleth in me, he doeth the works. 11 Believe me that I am in the Father, and the Father in me: or else believe me for the very works' sake. (KJV)

John 14:12 Verily, verily, I say unto you, He that believeth on me, the works that I do shall he do also; and greater works than these shall he do; because I go unto my Father.

John 14:13 And whatsoever ye shall ask in my name, that will I do, that the Father may be glorified in the Son. 14 If ye shall ask any thing in my name, I will do it. (KJV)

John 15:1 I am the true vine, and my Father is the husbandman. **(KJV)**

John 15:4 Abide in me, and I in you. As the branch cannot bear fruit of itself, except it abide in the vine; no more can ye, except ye abide in me. **(KJV)**

John 15:5 I am the vine, ye are the branches: He that abideth in me, and I in him, the same bringeth forth much fruit: for without me ye can do nothing 7 If ye abide in me, and my words abide in you, ye shall ask what ye will, and it shall be done unto you. **(KJV)**

John 15:8 Herein is my Father glorified, that ye bear much fruit; so shall ye be my disciples. 9 As the Father hath loved me, so have I loved you: continue ye in my love. **(KJV)**

John 15:10 If ye keep my commandments, ye shall abide in my love; even as I have kept my Father's commandments, and abide in his love. 11 These things have I spoken unto you, that my joy might remain in you, and that your joy might be full. **(KJV)**

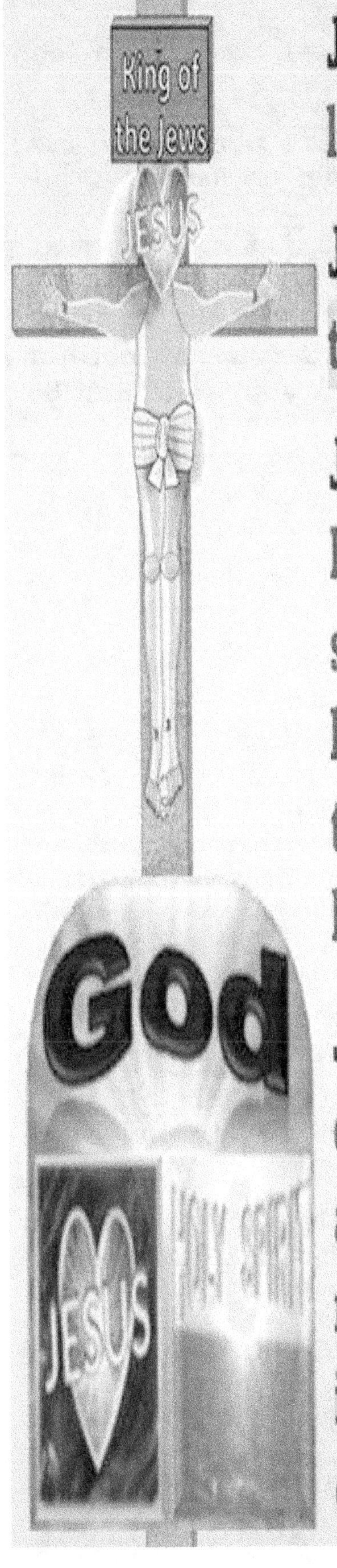

John 15:12 This is my commandment, That ye love one another, as I have loved you. **(KJV)**

John 15:13 Greater love hath no man than this, that a man lay down his life for his friends. **(KJV)**

John 15:14 Ye are my friends, if ye do whatsoever I command you. **15** Henceforth I call you not servants; for the servant knoweth not what his lord doeth: but I have called you friends; for all things that I have heard of my Father I have made known unto you. **(KJV)**

John 15:16 Ye have not chosen me, but I have chosen you, and ordained you, that ye should go and bring forth fruit, and that your fruit should remain: that whatsoever ye shall ask of the Father in my name, he may give it you. **17** These things I command you, that ye love one another. **(KJV)**

The Disciples listened carefully to their Master. They heard Jesus say, in **John 14:15**, "If ye love me, keep my commandments."

Now that Judas Iscariot was no longer in the room, they felt sure every man loved Jesus. They probably thought, "**Yes, we all do a fine job keeping Jesus' commandments.**"

John 14:16 And I will pray the Father, and he shall give you another Comforter, that he may abide with you for ever; 17 Even the Spirit of truth; whom the world cannot receive, because it seeth him not, neither knoweth him: but ye know him; for he dwelleth with you, and shall be in you. (KJV)

In **John 14:16**, they heard this news with surprise. What? Jesus will ask His Father to give us another Comforter who will abide with us forever. Does He mean forever or just for a few years? Also, does He mean a new teacher will step into His place? I feel confused."

That feeling of confusion grew and made many of them feel all twisted up inside as they strived to comprehend His following words.

Jesus said, in **John 14:18**, "I will not leave you comfortless: I will come to you. 19 Yet a little while, and the world seeth me no more; but ye see me: because I live, ye shall live also. 20 At that day ye shall know that I am in my Father, and ye in me, and I in you. 21 He that hath my commandments, and keepeth them, he it is that loveth me: and he that loveth me shall be loved of my Father, and I will love him, and will manifest myself to him."

The other Judas, who usually went by Thaddeus, could no longer keep quiet. In **John 14:22**, he asked, "**Lord, how is it that thou wilt manifest thyself unto us, and not unto the world?**"

Jesus' answer confused them even more. They heard him say, in **John 14:23**, "If a man love me, he will keep my words: and my Father will love him, and we will come unto him, and make our abode with him."

They probably thought, "**Abode? Does he mean to say He and this Comforter will come live in our house? But whose house? Mine? His? Will He take turns?**"

Jesus continued. In **John 14:24**, He said, "He that loveth me not keepeth not my sayings: and the word which ye hear is not mine, but the Father's which sent me. 25 These things have I spoken unto you, being yet present with you. 26 But the **Comforter, which is the Holy Ghost**, whom the Father will send in my name, he shall teach you all things, and bring all things to your remembrance, whatsoever I have said unto you."

This may have been the first time they heard Jesus reference the **Holy Ghost**. They probably now understand the Comforter was not a literal person. But how did Jesus intend to send them this Spirit? When would it happen? How would it happen?

Jesus' following words helped ease that twisted feeling a bit when He said, in **John 14:27**, **"Peace I leave with you, my Peace I give unto you: not as the world giveth, give I unto you. Let not your heart be troubled, neither let it be afraid."**

Peace. If they allowed their mind chatter to calm down, they could sense a feeling of Peace filling the room. Ahhh! It almost felt like a warm bath. They found themselves basking in that flowing river of Peace.

But then, when Jesus reminded them He was departing, that peaceful feeling almost disappeared. They sadly listened as He said, "in **John 14:28**, **"Ye have heard how I said unto you, I go away, and come again unto you. If ye loved me, ye would rejoice, because I said, I go unto the Father: for my Father is greater than I. 29 And now I have told you before it come to pass, that, when it is come to pass, ye might believe."**

Then, the next thing Jesus said almost made them feel like an icy river was edging toward them. Using a lower voice tone, Jesus said, in **John 14:30**, "**Hereafter I will not talk much with you: for the prince of this world cometh, and hath nothing in me."**

What? Jesus just mentioned the devil like he might be in the room listening. The Disciples probably stared into the room's dark corners with a sense of fear.

Jesus ended with these words, in **John 14:31**, **"But that the world may know that I love the Father; and as the Father gave me commandment, even so I do."**

FYI - John 14:31 concludes with Jesus saying, "Arise, let us go hence."

But Jesus had some more things to share. He might have shared these words before this night or planned to share them on the Mount of Olives. But let's remain in the Upper Room a bit longer as we learn about the final two points covered by John in the chapters **John 15 and 16**.

6 (6) The Work of the Holy Spirit (John 15:26-27) and (John 16:1-15)

After Jesus taught His Disciples about the coming Comforter, whom He called the Holy Ghost, in **John 16:26**, Jesus said this: **"But when the Comforter is come, whom I will send unto you from the Father, , even the Spirit of truth, which proceedeth from the Father, he shall testify of me: 27 And ye also shall bear witness, because ye have been with me from the beginning."** (KJV)

With His next words, Jesus would be painting a picture of what the Disciples would soon face as they tried to share what they learned about and from Jesus. What they did not yet know was the following six things:

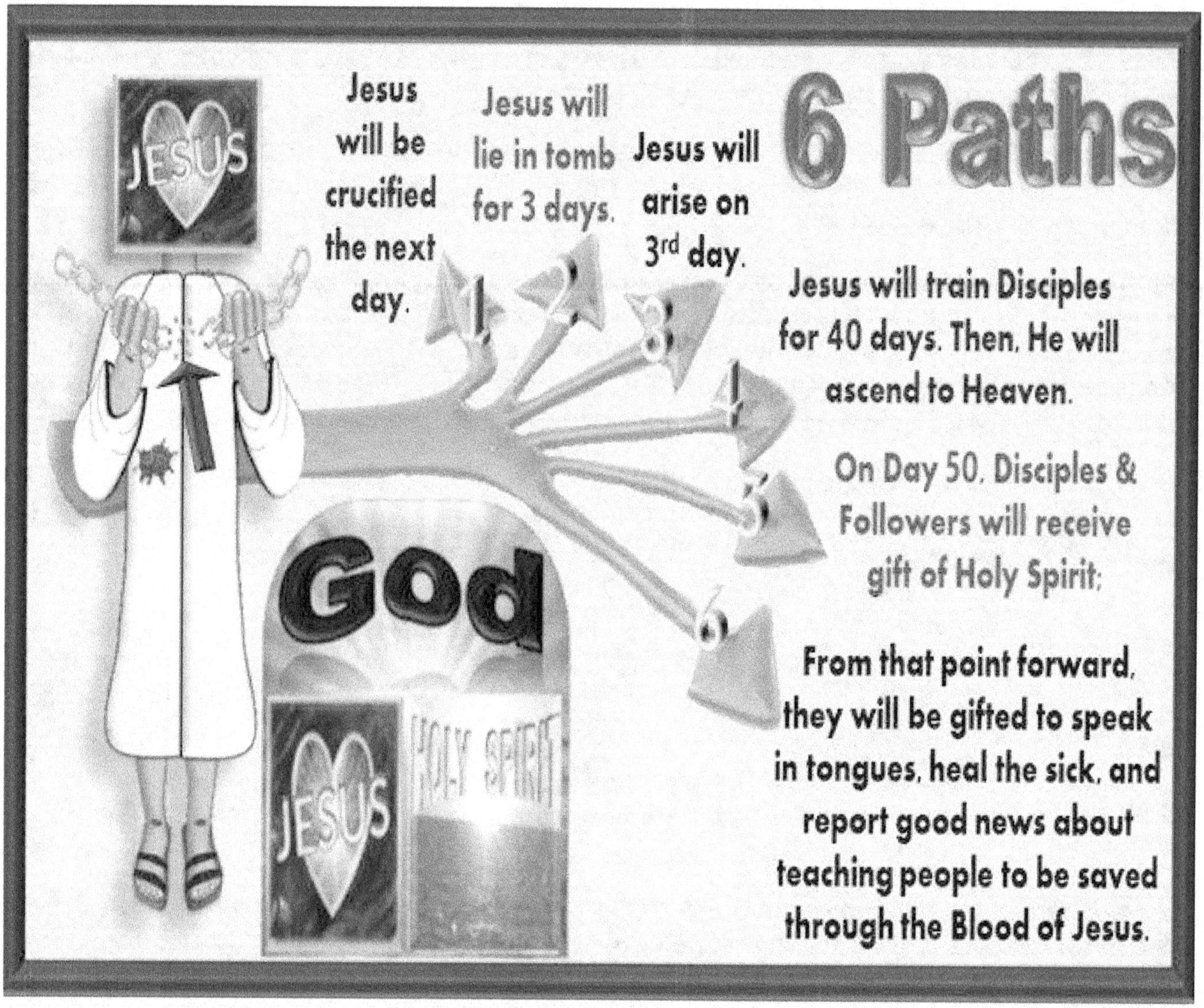

Jesus had some bad news to tell the Disciples. He introduced the topic, in **John 16:1**, by stating, "These things have I spoken unto you, that ye should not be offended." **(KJV)**

The Disciples listened carefully as Jesus gave them the alarming news. Jesus said, in **John 16:2**, "They shall put you out of the synagogues: yea, the time cometh, that whosoever killeth you will think that he doeth God service. 3 And these things will they do unto you, because they have not known the Father, nor me." **(KJV)**

This would be incredibly challenging for Peter, above all the other Disciples. Why? Before he met Jesus, he was known to be reckless and quick-tempered. Imagine this. Perhaps, two-by-two, the Disciples go into a synagogue to teach. Instead of being welcomed with open arms or ignored, they will hear these offending words: "You blasphemers! Get out of our Temple!"

Will you respond like Jesus, or will you allow Satan to dominate?
You blasphemers! Get out of our Temple?
Grrrrr! I would like to tell them a thing or two!
Aha! They're failing as His followers!

The Disciples have two choices. They can **respond like Jesus** as they kindly, calmly, and respectfully leave the synagogue. Or they can allow their **FIGHT OR FLIGHT trauma response to activate**. They might fire back with rude, loud, and disrespectful words or threats. They might stomp out of the synagogue with glaring facial expressions. They could ignore all the lessons they learned over the previous three years and play right into Satan's eager hands.

When the Disciples were aggressively accused of being blasphemers, this would **TRIGGER** the neurotransmitters in their brains. Before meeting Jesus, their **ROUTINE** would be to out-yell, out-threaten, and even use their fists to forcefully make their point. They would receive a positive **REWARD** of a feeling of satisfaction if they won the argument or fight. They would receive a negative **REWARD** if they lost the fight, got stoned, were imprisoned, or received some other negative consequence.

Jesus had tried hard to teach His Disciples a new way of responding to trauma. But without Jesus being present in the physical, would they be able to stick to their training? Would they maintain their calm knowing that the **Holy Spirit** would be with them, offering quiet advice and aid? That would likely be a frequent challenge.

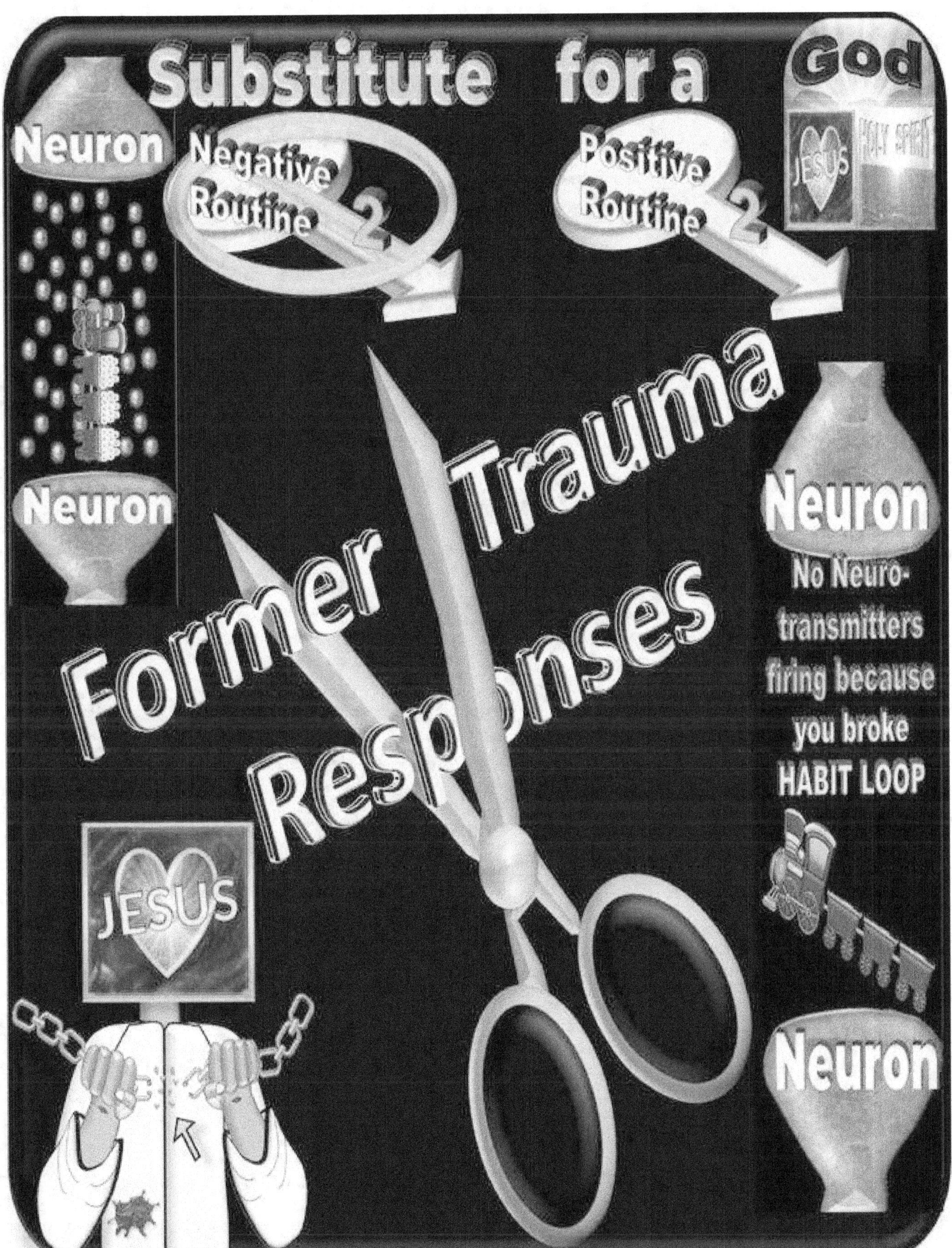

Substitute for a
Neuron
Negative Routine 2
Positive Routine 2
God
JESUS
HOLY SPIRIT
Neuron
Former Trauma Responses
Neuron
No Neuro-transmitters firing because you broke HABIT LOOP
JESUS
Neuron

Will you respond like Jesus, or will you allow Satan to dominate?
You blasphemers! Get out of our Temple?
HOLY SPIRIT
JESUS
We're covered by the BLOOD of our Lord Jesus!

Jesus continued with His warning words. In **John 16:4**, He stated, "But these things have I told you, that when the time shall come, ye may remember that I told you of them. And these things I said not unto you at the beginning, because I was with you." (KJV)

In other words, while Jesus was still alive, He could somewhat keep them safe as He, part of the **Triune God**, could watch over them. He could act the part of a Mother Hen sheltering them under His protective wings. But it would be much more challenging for them after His ascension.

Jesus continued in **John 16:5** But now I go my way to him that sent me; and none of you asketh me, Whither goest thou?

John 16:6 But because I have said these things unto you, sorrow hath filled your heart.

John 16:7 Nevertheless I tell you the truth; It is expedient for you that I go away: for if I go not away, the Comforter will not come unto you; but if I depart, I will send him unto you. **(KJV)**

In **John 16:8 to 16:15**, Jesus describes seven of the benefits the Disciples will receive when they get the Holy Spirit: He begins this description in **John 16:8** by saying, "And when he is come, ..." Here is that 7-part list.

Holy Spirit Benefits

1

Jesus said: He will reprove the world of sin, and of righteousness, and of judgment. (John 16:8)

2
Jesus said: Of sin, because they believe not on me. (John 16:9)

3

Jesus said: Of righteousness, because I go to my Father, and ye see me no more. (John 16:10)

4
Jesus said: Of judgment, because the prince of this world is judged. (John 16:11)

5

Jesus said: Howbeit when he, the Spirit of truth, is come, he will guide you into all truth: for he shall not speak of himself; but whatsoever he shall hear, that shall he speak: and he will shew you things to come. (John 16:13)

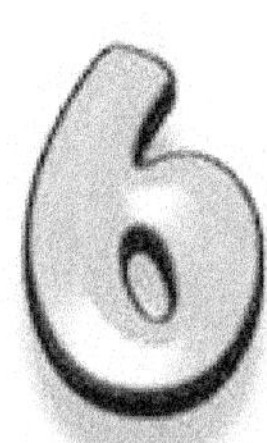

6

Jesus said: He shall glorify me: for he shall receive of mine, and shall shew it unto you. (John 16:14)

7

Jesus said: All things that the Father hath are mine: therefore said I, that he shall take of mine, and shall shew it unto you. (John 16:15)

John 16:12 I have yet many things to say unto you, but ye cannot bear them now. (KJV)

These are the final words that Jesus had to share with His Disciples before they headed off to the garden. That is where He would pray, encounter Judas Iscariot and His fellow betrayers, get arrested, and then be led off to be questioned, tried, beaten, tortured, and then crucified.

Not only had it been a long evening with much ground covered, but the Disciples were likely feeling tired. So, when Jesus began speaking even more mysteriously, they began to feel all twisted up inside again.

John 16:17 **Then said some of his disciples among themselves, What is this that he saith unto us, A little while, and ye shall not see me: and again, a little while, and ye shall see me: and, Because I go to the Father?** (KJV)

John 16:18 **They said therefore, What is this that he saith, A little while? we cannot tell what he saith.** (KJV)

John 16:19 **Now Jesus knew that they were desirous to ask him, and said unto them,** Do ye enquire among yourselves of that I said, A little while, and ye shall not see me: and again, a little while, and ye shall see me? (KJV)

John 16:20 Verily, verily, I say unto you, That ye shall weep and lament, but the world shall rejoice: and ye shall be sorrowful, but your sorrow shall be turned into joy. (KJV)

John 16:21 A woman when she is in travail hath sorrow, because her hour is come: but as soon as she is delivered of the child, she remembereth no more the anguish, for joy that a man is born into the world. (KJV)

John 16:22 And ye now therefore have sorrow: but I will see you again, and your heart shall rejoice, and your joy no man taketh from you.

God

John 16:23 And in that day ye shall ask me nothing. Verily, verily, I say unto you, Whatsoever ye shall ask the Father in my name, he will give it you.

John 16:24 Hitherto have ye asked nothing in my name: ask, and ye shall receive, that your joy may be full . (KJV)

John 16:25 These things have I spoken unto you in proverbs: but the time cometh, when I shall no more speak unto you in proverbs, but I shall shew you plainly of the Father.

John 16:26 At that day ye shall ask in my name: and I say not unto you, that I will pray the Father for you: 27 For the Father himself loveth you, because ye have loved me, and have believed that I came out from God. 28 I came forth from the Father, and am come into the world: again, I leave the world, and go to the Father. (KJV)

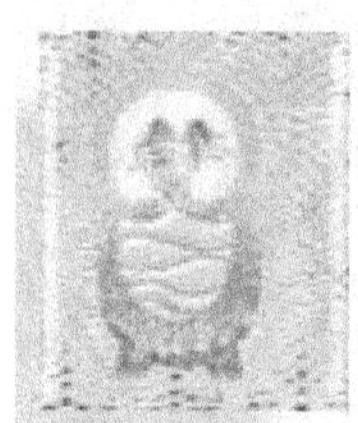

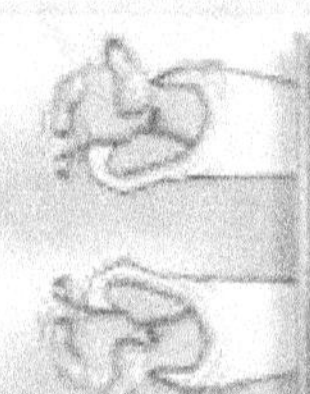

John 16:29 **His disciples said unto him, Lo, now speakest thou plainly, and speakest no proverb.** (KJV)

John 16:30 **Now are we sure that thou knowest all things, and needest not that any man should ask thee: by this we believe that thou camest forth from God.** (KJV)

John 16:31 **Jesus answered them,** Do ye now believe?

John 16:32 Behold, the hour cometh, yea, is now come, that ye shall be scattered, every man to his own, and shall leave me alone: and yet I am not alone, because the Father is with me. (KJV)

John 16:33 These things I have spoken unto you, that in me ye might have peace. In the world ye shall have tribulation: but be of good cheer; I have overcome the world. **(KJV)**

Matthew 26:30	Mark 14:26	Luke 22:39	John 14:31
30 And when they had sung a hymn, they went out into the **mount of Olives**.	26 And when they had sung a hymn, they went out into the **mount of Olives**.	39 And he came out, and went, as he was wont, to the **mount of Olives**; and his disciples also followed him.	31 But that the world may know that I love the Father; and as the Father gave me commandment, even so I do. Arise, let us go hence.

Wikipedia quote

Is the Mount of Olives near the Garden of Gethsemane?

"Gethsemane is a garden at the foot of the Mount of Olives in East Jerusalem where, according to the four Gospels of the New Testament, Jesus Christ underwent the agony in the garden and was arrested before his crucifixion."

JERUSALEM & OTHER KEY AREAS

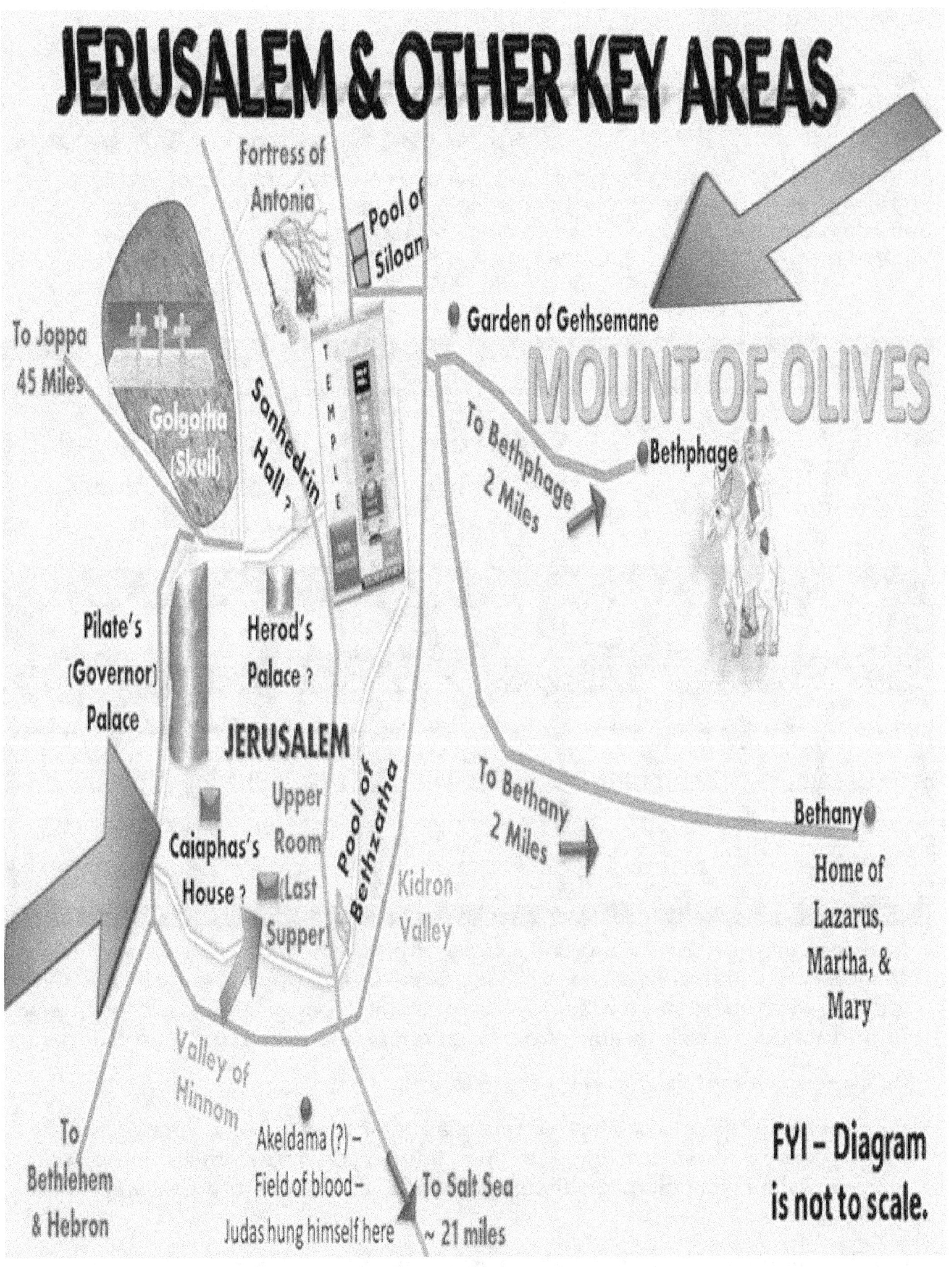

Thursday – Last Supper, Garden of Gethsemane, & Jesus arrested at midnight
Friday – Crucifixion & Jesus' body placed in a rich man's tomb
Saturday (Sabbath) – While eleven remaining Disciples hide in Upper Room
11 Disciples: (1) Andrew, (2) Bartholomew, (3) Matthew, (4) Simon the Zealot, (5) Thaddaeus, (6) Thomas, (7) Philip, (8) Little James, (9) Big James Z., (10) John Z., and (11) Peter

1. Imagine that on that Saturday, Mary, the mother of Jesus, and Mary Magdalene came to see you, the Disciples, in the Upper Room. After they shared what they saw on Friday, both women begged to learn as many important details as possible about what happened during the Last Supper.

   A. Choose which Disciple you will represent.

   B. Either journal your answer or role-play your answer as a group. Tell the two Marys about the three to five things you found most interesting, meaningful, touching, or disturbing about that Thursday evening's Last Supper.

   C. See the ten points above to help you frame your answer.

Author's Dedication

There are many ways to demonstrate our love for and worship of our Lord Jesus Christ. This book is a rendering of data points for you to prayerfully consider that might give your worship of Him a deeper dimension. I dedicate this book to all honest seekers of truth. May it provide another viewing point of the **WORD** in the Holy Bible.

Author's Acknowledgements

There was a deeper purpose for authoring this book. I wrote this book not for my glory but for the glory of our Heavenly God the Father, God the Son, and God the Holy Spirit. I am so grateful for all the manifold ways God, the **Trinity of three Persons**, continually blesses my life. May this book bless your life, as well.

I acknowledge and am so grateful for all the people who created the Bible APPS, Google, Microsoft PowerPoint, Microsoft Word, the Paint APP, books, videos, movies, talks, and sermons that fed my imagination and blessed my life. I also acknowledge the countless moments of comfort and blessings I receive from my dear and treasured family and friends (both living and deceased), of which I count you, my readers, among them. I am eternally grateful! God bless you all! May you have a blessed and touched-by-God life!

Final Blessings

I find myself speculating if God planted me exactly where He did and gave me all the experiences that He gave me just so I could write this book.

And then I feel the **Holy Spirit** nudging me, reminding me of this Bible verse:

Romans 8:28 And we know that all things work together for good to them that love God, to them who are called according to his purpose. (KJV)

May the **Holy Spirit** touch and bless you, as well, and help you to fulfill the mission that God has prescribed just for you.

I end this book with two final blessings, one by King David, the other by Moses.

Psalm 121:8 The Lord keeps watch over you as you come and go, both now and forever. (NLT)

Numbers 6:24 The LORD bless you and keep you. 25 The LORD make his face shine upon you and be gracious to you. 26 The LORD turn his face toward you and give you peace. (NIV)

AMEN. Thank you for making the time to read a part or all of this book. Kindly consider leaving a review, even if it is only a sentence or two.

Also, if you found it pleasing, please share this book with the people you love.

BIBLIOGRAPHY

Bibliography: Used for entire book

Bible Gateway.com. (October 2023 to April 2024). Read the Bible. Website; https://www.biblegateway.com/

Developer Unknown. (October 2023 to April 2024). Bible – Daily Bible Verse KJV. From a free cell phone APP.

Google.com Search Engine. (October 2023 to April 2024).

Grammarly.com for editing (October 2023 to April 2024).

Kairos Software LLC. Developer. (October 2023 to April 2024). Bible KJV Strong's Concordance. From a free cell phone APP. (October – November 2023)

On-line dictionary via Google Search Engine. (October 2023 to April 2024).

Bibliography: Resources to increase my understanding

Asia News.it of the PIME missionaries. (January 2024). Pope: Christ is the true sacrificial lamb of the Last Supper. Website: https://www.asianews.it/index.php?l=en&art=8936&size=A

Barrett, David P. for Bible Mapper.com. (December 2023). Bethany and Bethphage. Website: https://biblemapper.com/blog/index.php/2020/04/04/bethany-and-bethphage/

Blue Letter Bible. (November 2023). David Guzik: Study Guide for Zechariah 11. Website: https://www.blueletterbible.org/comm/guzik_david/study-guide/zechariah/zechariah-11.cfm

Brain Facts.org. (December 2023). How Many Neurons Are in the Brain? Website: https://www.brainfacts.org/in-the-lab/meet-the-researcher/2018/how-many-neurons-are-in-the-brain-120418

Brindle, Wayne for Liberty University (March 2024). The Census and Quirinius: Luke 2:2. Website: https://digitalcommons.liberty.edu/cgi/viewcontent.cgi?article=1072&context=sor_fac_pubs

Brownell, Dan. (November 2023). Jesus in the Old Testament. Website: https://pointmetojesus.com/jesus-in-the-old-testament/

Calahan, John for Never Thirsty.org. (January 2024). On what day of the Jewish calendar does Passover begin? Website: https://www.neverthirsty.org/bible-qa/qa-archives/question/on-what-day-of-the-jewish-calendar-does-passover-begin/

Edwards, William D. (December 2023). Map of Jerusalem at time of Christ. Website: https://www.researchgate.net/figure/Map-of-Jerusalem-at-time-of-Christ-Jesus-left-Upper-Room-and-walked-with-disciples-to_fig1_19648788

Got Questions.org. (January 2024). If Jesus was crucified on the Day of Preparation, why had He already eaten the Passover meal? Website: https://www.gotquestions.org/Day-of-Preparation.html

Got Questions.org. (January 2024). What did Jesus mean when He said we must eat His flesh and drink His blood? Website: https://www.gotquestions.org/Jesus-eat-flesh-drink-blood.html

Got Questions.org. (November 2023). What is the significance of thirty pieces of silver? Website: https://www.gotquestions.org/thirty-pieces-of-silver.html

Grace Transcending the Torah.com. (April 2024). Feasts of the Lord. Website: https://www.gracetranscendingthetorah.com/feasts/

Michiels, Jordan Blake. (April 2024). Timeline: The Last Passover With Jesus. Website: https://www.linkedin.com/pulse/timeline-last-passover-jesus-jordan-blake-michiels

New World Translation of the Holy Scriptures. (December 2023). Jerusalem and Surrounding Area. Website: https://wol.jw.org/en/wol/pc/r1/lp-e/2023246/1/0

Passion for Truth Ministries on YouTube. (April 2024). The Connection to Passover to Pentecost - Jim Staley. Website: https://youtu.be/1_1uj6EX1co?si=-ivCqj2clKJSdiSb

Ramgopal and Arte for Presentation Process. (November 2023). How To Create Beautiful Chain Graphic in PowerPoint. Website: https://www.youtube.com/watch?v=jjioPJ-_glk

The Bible Nerds. (December 2023). Remez: A Hint For Better Bible Study. Website: https://thebiblenerds.com/remez-a-hint-for-better-bible-study/

Wikipedia.org. (March 2024). Judas Iscariot. Website: https://en.wikipedia.org/wiki/Judas_Iscariot

Wikipedia.org. (November 2023). Old Testament messianic prophecies quoted in the New Testament. Website: https://en.wikipedia.org/wiki/Old_Testament_messianic_prophecies_quoted_in_the_New_Testament

Winger, Mike on YouTube. (April 2024). The Spring Feasts of Israel: How to Find Jesus in the OT pt 21. Website: https://youtu.be/A-_6rpQ4zLg?si=ifsM5bWnjma82pH0